SCIENCE WHIZ
EXPERIMENTS

EXPERIMENTS WITH WEATHER

Robert Gardner

Enslow Publishing
100 W. 23rd Street
Suite 240
New York, NY 10011
USA

enslow.com

Published in 2018 by Enslow Publishing, LLC.
101 W. 23rd Street, Suite 240, New York, NY 10011

Library of Congress Cataloging-in-Publication Data

Names: Gardner, Robert, 1929- author.
Title: Experiments with weather / Robert Gardner.
Description: New York : Enslow Publishing, 2018. | Series: Science whiz experiments | Includes bibliographical references and index. | Audience: Grades 5-8.
Identifiers: LCCN 2017001921 | ISBN 9780766086869 (library-bound)
Subjects: LCSH: Weather--Experiments--Juvenile literature. | Weather--Juvenile literature.
Classification: LCC QC981.3 .G3793 2018 | DDC 551.5078--dc23
LC record available at https://lccn.loc.gov/2017001921

Printed in the United States of America

To Our Readers: We have done our best to make sure all website addresses in this book were active and appropriate when we went to press. However, the author and the publisher have no control over and assume no liability for the material available on those websites or on any websites they may link to. Any comments or suggestions can be sent by email to customerservice@enslow.com.

Illustrations by Joseph Hill
Photo Credits: Cover, p. 1, Dark Moon Pictures/Shutterstock.com; back cover and interior pages background pattern curiosity/Shutterstock.com.

Contents

Introduction. 5

Chapter 1

The Pressure of Air. 9

1.1   Air Pressure 12
1.2   The Weight of Air 15
1.3   Torricelli's Barometer. 17
1.4   Air Pressure and Altitude 20
1.5   An Aneroid Barometer 22

Chapter 2

Rain. 25

2.1   The Water Cycle 27
2.2   Measuring Raindrops. 28
2.3   Tiny Droplets Grow Larger 30
2.4   Falling Raindrops 32
2.5   Terminal Velocity 34
2.6   Snowflakes. 36
2.7   Build a Rain Gauge. 38
2.8   How Much Water Is in Snow? 41

Chapter 3

Weather Instruments. 42

3.1   A Thermometer 43
3.2   Graphing the Temperature. 47
3.3   A Look at Wind 49
3.4   Wind Speed. 52
3.5   Relative Humidity 55
3.6   Dew Points and Absolute Humidity. 59

Chapter 4

Wind and Sky. 62

4.1   Can You Make a Cloud?. 64
4.2   Can You Make Fog? 66

4.3   Temperature Effects on Air 67

4.4   Density Effects on the Atmosphere 68

4.5   Sun and the Seasons 70

4.6   A Look at Rainbows 72

4.7   Reading a Weather Map 78

4.8   The Sun Heats Earth 79

4.9   How the Wind Blows................................. 82

4.10   Winds on Planet Earth 83

Chapter 5

Climate Change

Climate Change 86

5.1   Glaciers and Sea Ice................................. 87

5.2   A Greenhouse Gas 91

5.3   Carbon Dioxide and Seas 95

5.4   Evaporation and Global Warming 96

5.5   Polar Regions and Global Warming 97

5.6   Clouds, Volcanoes, and Earth's Temperature......... 100

Appendix: Science Supply Companies 104

Glossary 105

Further Reading 108

Index 110

Introduction

The weather seems to be a topic that people talk about quite often. You have probably overheard these common sayings, or have said them yourself: "How is the weather?" "Is it going to rain tomorrow?" "I hope we have nice weather on our vacation!" The science behind the weather is quite fascinating, and by doing experiments, you will discover the forces that affect the weather. It is more fun to learn about weather with hands-on activities than by simply reading about it.

At times, as you experiment, you may need a partner to help you. Try to work with someone who enjoys experimenting as much as you do. If any danger is involved in doing an experiment, it will be made known to you. **In some cases, to avoid danger, you will be asked to work with an adult. Please do so.** Do not take any chances that could lead to an injury.

Like any good scientist, you will find it useful to record your ideas, procedures, data, and conclusions in a notebook. Your record will likely help you in doing later projects.

Entering a Science Fair

Some of the investigations in this book contain ideas you might use at a science fair. However, judges at science fairs do not reward projects or experiments that are simply copied from a book. A model of clouds made from white cotton stuck on cardboard would not impress most judges; however, finding unique ways to measure the heat released when water vapor condenses into rain would attract their attention.

Science fair judges tend to reward creative thought and imagination. It is difficult to be creative or imaginative unless you are really interested in your project; therefore, try to choose an investigation that appeals to you. And before you jump into a project, also consider your own talents and the cost of the materials you will need.

If you decide to use an experiment or idea found in this book for a science fair, you should find ways to modify or extend it. This should not be difficult because you will discover that as you carry out investigations, new ideas come to mind. Ideas will come to you that could make excellent science fair projects, particularly because the ideas are your own and are interesting to you.

If you decide to enter a science fair and have never done so, you should read some of the books listed in the Further Reading section. These books deal specifically with science fairs and provide plenty of helpful hints and useful information that will enable you to avoid the pitfalls that sometimes plague first-time entrants. You will learn how to prepare appealing reports that include charts and graphs, how to set up and display your work, how to present your project, and how to relate to judges and visitors.

Be Safe

Most of the projects included in this book are perfectly safe. However, the following safety rules are well worth reading before you start any project.

1. **Never experiment with flames or electrical appliances without adult supervision.**
2. Do any experiments or projects, whether from this book or of your own design, under the supervision of a science teacher or other knowledgeable adult.
3. Read all instructions carefully before proceeding with a project. If you have questions, check with your supervisor before going any further.
4. Maintain a serious attitude while conducting experiments. Fooling around can be dangerous to you and others.
5. Wear approved safety goggles when you are working with a flame or doing anything that might cause injury to your eyes.

6. Have a first-aid kit nearby while you are experimenting.
7. Do not put your fingers or any object other than properly designed electrical connectors into electrical outlets.
8. Never let water droplets come in contact with a hot lightbulb.
9. Use only digital or alcohol-based thermometers. Some older thermometers contain mercury, which is a dangerous substance.

Following the Scientific Method

Scientists look at the world and try to understand how things work. They make careful observations and conduct research. Different areas of science use different approaches. Depending on the problem, one method is likely to be better than another. Designing a new medicine for heart disease; studying the spread of an invasive plant, such as purple loosestrife; and finding evidence of water on Mars all require different methods.

Despite the differences, all scientists use a similar general approach in doing experiments. This is called the scientific method. In most experiments, some or all of the following steps are used: observing a problem, formulating a question, making a hypothesis (an answer to the question), making a prediction (an if-then statement), designing and conducting an experiment, analyzing results, drawing conclusions, and accepting or rejecting the hypothesis. Scientists then share their findings by writing articles that are published.

You might wonder how to start an experiment. When you observe something, you may become curious and ask a question. Your question, which could arise from an earlier experiment or from reading, may be answered by a well-designed investigation. Once you have a question, you can make a hypothesis. Your hypothesis is a possible answer to the question. Once you have a hypothesis, it is time to design an experiment to test a consequence of your hypothesis.

In most cases, you should do a controlled experiment. This means having two groups that are treated the same except for the one factor being tested. That factor is called a variable. For example, suppose your question is "Do green plants need light?" Your hypothesis might be that they do need light. To test the hypothesis, you would use two groups of green plants. One group is called the control group; the other is called the experimental group. The two groups should be treated the same except for one factor. Both should be planted in the same amount and type of soil, given the same amount of water, kept at the same temperature, and so forth. The control group would be placed in the dark. The experimental group would be put in the light. Light is the variable. It is the only difference between the two groups.

During the experiment, you would collect data. For example, you might measure the plants' growth in centimeters, count the number of living and dead leaves, and note the color and condition of the leaves. By comparing the data collected from the control and experimental groups over a few weeks, you would draw conclusions. Healthier growth and survival rates of plants grown in light would allow you to conclude that green plants need light.

Two other terms are often used in scientific experiments—dependent and independent variables. One dependent variable in this example is healthy growth, which depends on light being present. Light is the independent variable. It does not depend on anything.

After the data are collected, they are analyzed to see if they support or reject the hypothesis. The results of one experiment often lead you to a related question. Or they may send you off in a different direction. Whatever the results, something can be learned from every experiment.

Chapter 1

The Pressure of Air

Have you ever jumped deep into a pool and felt some pressure on your ears? Or perhaps you noticed ear pressure gets greater as you drop deeper under the water. That is because the water pressure increases the deeper you go. Submarine hulls must be very strong to withstand the pressure deep in the ocean. This pressure is caused by the weight of the water.

We all live at the bottom of another ocean—a sea of air more than 100 km (60 mi) deep. Most of the air is within 10 km (6 mi) of Earth's surface. If the sea we live in were water, the pressure would be huge. But air weighs much less than water, so we live comfortably at the bottom of our sea of air.

As you will see, air pressure is very much a part of weather and weather predictions. Consequently, you need an instrument that measures air pressure. That instrument is a barometer. It measures the pressure of a column of air extending from Earth's surface to the top of the atmosphere. At sea level, that pressure is equal to that of a column of water 10 m (33 ft) deep.

In 1643, an Italian physicist, Evangelista Torricelli (1608–1647), built the world's first barometer (Figure 1a). Torricelli sealed one end of a narrow 1.2-meter-long glass tube and filled it with mercury. He put his thumb over the open end of the tube and inverted it. He placed the tube's end in a dish of mercury and removed his thumb. The mercury began to empty into the dish. It stopped emptying when the mercury level in the tube was 76 cm (30 in) above the mercury in the dish. This left an empty space at the top of the tube. Torricelli reasoned that the empty space was a vacuum because no air bubbles had gone up the tube. He realized that the weight of the mercury pushing downward at the mouth

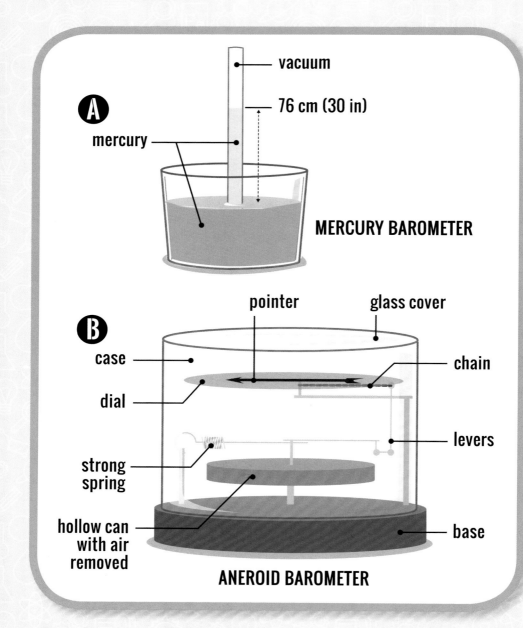

A

vacuum

76 cm (30 in)

mercury

MERCURY BAROMETER

B

pointer

glass cover

case

chain

dial

levers

strong spring

hollow can with air removed

base

ANEROID BAROMETER

Figure 1 a) This mercury barometer is similar to Torricelli's. b) An aneroid barometer like this one requires no mercury. The hollow, evacuated can in an aneroid barometer is squeezed by air pressure. Changes in air pressure cause the can to expand or contract. These changes are magnified by levers that are connected to a pointer by a chain. The pointer moves over a dial, shown above, that allows you to read the air pressure.

of the tube was balanced by the pressure of the air pushing upward. (Air exerts pressure in all directions–up, down, and sideways.)

Meteorologists still measure air pressure by the height of mercury in a barometer. A mercury height of 76 cm (30 in) is normal air pressure at sea level.

Meteorologists may express air pressure in millibars instead of centimeters or inches of mercury. Air pressure at sea level is 1,030 millibars, which is about the same as 10 Newtons/cm² (N/cm^2).

Mercury is expensive and its vapors are poisonous. Therefore, you will use an aneroid barometer (Figure 1b). It contains no mercury. But before you work with a barometer, let's understand how an aneroid barometer works. Let's also examine a famous experiment and show that air has weight.

1.1 Air Pressure

Otto von Guericke (1602–1686) was a German physicist. He became the mayor of Magdeburg, the city where he was born. He questioned something proposed by Aristotle, an ancient Greek philosopher. Aristotle said that it was impossible to create a vacuum—an empty space where the pressure is zero. Von Guericke decided to test Aristotle's assumption by doing an experiment that became famous.

He built a pump, which we call a vacuum pump. This pump could remove air in the same way that a water pump can remove water from a well. Being somewhat of a showman, he built two large, hollow bronze hemispheres. They fit together very well (Figure 2a). Von Guericke then used his air pump to evacuate, or remove air from, the space inside the joined hemispheres, known as the Magdeburg hemispheres. Von Guericke reasoned that because there was no air pressure inside, air pressure on the outside would hold the hemispheres together.

To test his hypothesis, he had several men try to pull the hemispheres apart. They could not. Confident that his hypothesis was correct, he invited Emperor Ferdinand III to a demonstration. He hitched two eight-horse teams to opposite hemispheres. Pull as they might, the horses could not pull the hemispheres apart.

When von Guericke learned of Torricelli's barometer, he realized that a force of more than 7 tons pushed on each hemisphere. It is no wonder that the horses were unsuccessful.

You can do a miniature version of von Guericke's experiment.

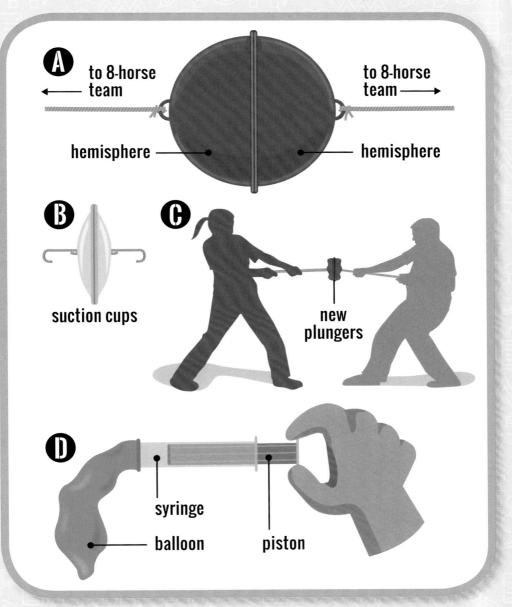

Figure 2. a) Otto von Guericke's experiment. b) A miniature version of von Guericke's experiment. c) An enlarged version of the experiment. d) How an air pump works.

1. Press two suction cups firmly together to squeeze out any air between them (Figure 2b).
2. Try to pull them apart. Why is it so difficult?

   If you have a pair of new toilet plungers, you can do the same experiment on a larger scale.
3. Wet the rims of the plungers.
4. Together with a partner, press the plungers together. Then try to pull them apart (Figure 2c). Why is it more difficult than pulling the suction cups apart?
5. You can see how von Guericke's vacuum pump worked. Attach an uninflated balloon to a syringe (Figure 2d). The piston should be as far into the cylinder as it can go. Slowly pull the piston out. What happens to the balloon?

   Von Guericke's pump had one-way valves. These valves allowed him to pump air from the sphere without disconnecting the pump.

1.2 The Weight of Air

If air has weight, you should be able to weigh it. One way would be to use a vacuum pump to evacuate a sturdy can. You could then weigh the airless can, let the air back in, and reweigh it. The difference in weight would be due to the air. Lacking a vacuum pump, you can show that air has weight in a different way.

1. Let all the air out of a basketball or soccer ball, but do not squeeze it together. Let it keep its round shape.

2. Weigh the ball on a laboratory balance. Record the weight.

3. Next, pump air into the ball until it is very hard. Then weigh the ball again. Record its weight when inflated. How can you tell that air has weight?

IDEAS
FOR A SCIENCE FAIR PROJECT

- **With adult supervision**, use a vacuum pump to remove the air from a sturdy can that has a spout. Weigh the evacuated can. Let air back into the can and reweigh it. How much did the air weigh? How can you find the density of the air? How would changes in air pressure affect the density?

- **With adult supervision**, find the density of other gases, such as carbon dioxide, oxygen, nitrogen, and helium.

1.3 Torricelli's Barometer

This experiment will enable you to see how air pressure affects a barometer.

1. Find a clear plastic container with a tight-fitting cover that can hold about 500 mL (1 pint) of water.

2. **Ask an adult** to use a sharp knife to make small perpendicular slits in two places near opposite sides of the cover (Figure 3a).

3. Insert a plastic soda straw a short distance through one set of slits. Insert a wider, clear plastic straw through the second set of slits.

4. Seal the small openings around the straws with soft clay. See Figure 3b.

5. Fill about three-fourths of the container with water. Add a few drops of food coloring to improve visibility.

6. Put the cover on the container. The end of the wide straw should extend below the water level in the container. The end of the narrower straw should be above the water (Figure 3c). Adjust straws if necessary and reseal.

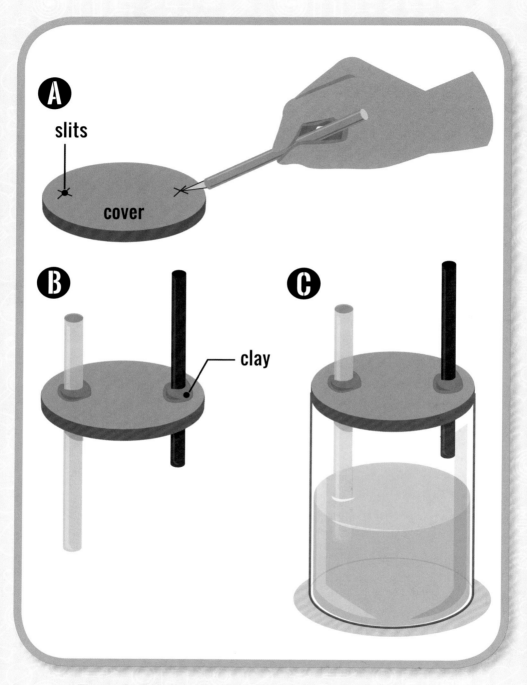

Figure 3. This is one way to show how a mercury barometer works.

7. Put your lips around the narrower straw. Use your mouth to force air into the space above the water in the container. This will increase air pressure in the container. What happens to the water level in the wider straw?

8. Carefully reduce the air pressure inside the container by sucking a small amount of air from the container. What happens to the water level in the wider straw?

How does this experiment help you to understand how a mercury barometer works?

1.4 Air Pressure and Altitude

1. Obtain an aneroid barometer like the one shown in Figure 1b. It will work as well inside as outside because no building is airtight. Pressures inside and outside equalize quickly.

2. Record daily air pressure according to the barometer. At the same time, record the type of weather—fair and cool, cloudy and warm, rain and warm, snow and cold, etc. How is the barometer affected by the weather? When does it give high readings? When does it give low readings? How can changing air pressure be used to predict changes in weather?

    As you go up into the atmosphere, there is less air above you. Predict how air pressure will be affected as you move to a higher altitude.

3. To test your prediction, take your aneroid barometer to the basement of a building or the base of a hill. If possible, choose a tall building or hill. A skyscraper or mountain would be ideal.

4. Read the barometer carefully and record the air pressure.

5. Carry the barometer to the top floor of the building or top of the hill. Read the barometer carefully. Record the air pressure. Do the results agree with your prediction?

6. Take the barometer on an automobile ride. Compare air pressures at the top and bottom of hills or mountains. How does altitude affect air pressure?

7. Take along an unopened bag of potato chips on an airplane trip. Feel the bag at low and high altitudes. What do you notice about the bag's firmness at different altitudes? How can you explain what you observe? What else could change the bag's firmness?

IDEAS FOR A SCIENCE FAIR PROJECT

- Measure air pressure at different altitudes. Plot a graph of air pressure versus altitude. How can you use air pressure to measure altitude?

- Would you expect there to be a relationship between home runs hit and the altitude of a major league baseball park? Do some research to find out. Is there any relationship?

1.5 An Aneroid Barometer

The caption for Figure 1b explains how an aneroid barometer works. The series of levers make it difficult to see how changes in air pressure can move the pointer over the dial. This experiment will help you to see how changes in air pressure can move a pointer.

1. Using scissors, cut off the neck of a balloon.
2. Pull the remaining part of the balloon over the top of a wide drinking glass. Fasten it to the glass with a strong rubber band.
3. Put two drinking straws together. Squeeze the end of one and slide it into the other. Make one end of the straws into a pointer by cutting that end diagonally as shown in Figure 4a.
4. Tape the other end of the straws to the center of the balloon that covers the glass.
5. Make a scale using cardboard, a clothespin, a ruler, and a marking pen as shown in Figure 4b.

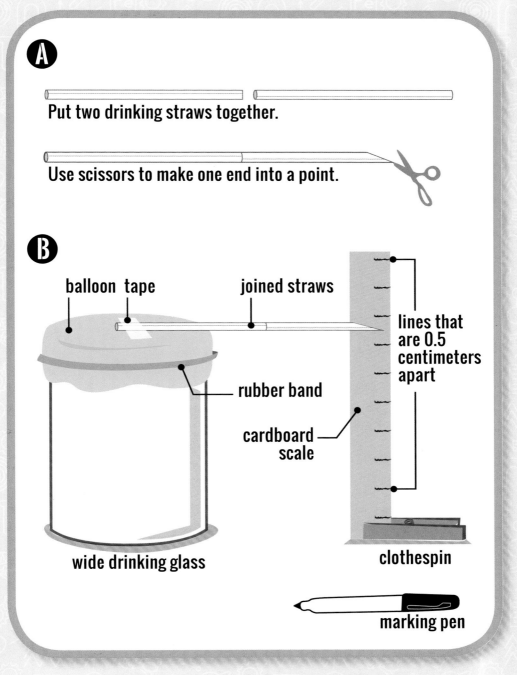

A

Put two drinking straws together.

Use scissors to make one end into a point.

B

balloon tape   joined straws

lines that are 0.5 centimeters apart

rubber band

cardboard scale

wide drinking glass

clothespin

marking pen

Figure 4. You can make a homemade aneroid barometer.

6. Put your homemade barometer in a place where the temperature remains relatively constant, such as a basement. Why should the temperature be constant? Hint: The working part of this barometer contains air.

7. Record the position of the pointer. Look at the position of the pointer every few hours for the next few days and record it in your notebook. Be sure to look when the weather is changing from fair to stormy or vice versa.

8. Compare the readings on your homemade barometer with those on a commercial aneroid barometer. How does the homemade barometer indicate increasing pressure? Decreasing pressure? How is your homemade barometer like a real aneroid barometer? How is it different?

Design and do an experiment to show how the volume of air is affected by temperature.

Design and do an experiment to show how the volume of air is affected by pressure.

Chapter 2

Rain

"Rain rain, go away, Come again another day." These lines are from a popular nursery rhyme. When rain falls on a day when you have an outdoor activity planned, you may not be very happy. But rain also fills our reservoirs for drinking water and supplies our food crops with needed moisture. Without rain, life could not exist.

People used to believe the fresh water found in lakes and ponds was seawater that had been filtered through the ground. Edmond Halley (1656–1742) was an English astronomer for whom a comet is named. He estimated the amount of water that evaporated from the Mediterranean Sea each year. He also estimated the river water that flowed into the same sea each year. The two estimates were equal. He reasoned correctly that the evaporated water had fallen as rain and then flowed back to the sea.

Careful measurements reveal that all the water that evaporates falls back to Earth as rain. There is, therefore, a water cycle (Figure 5).

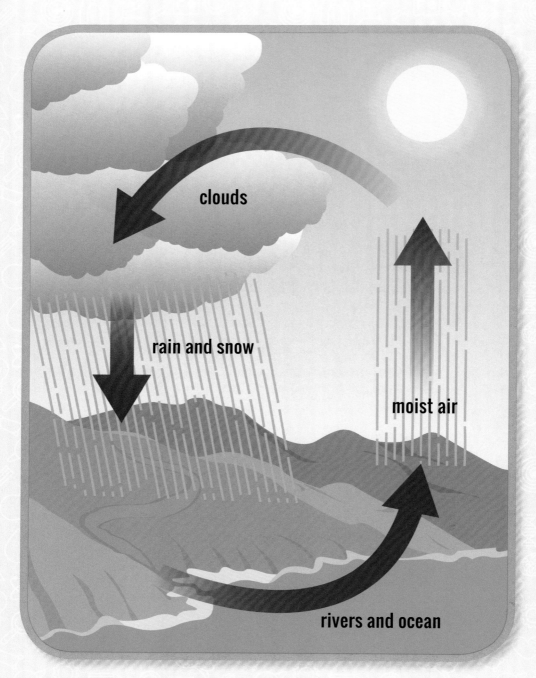

Figure 5. The water cycle: Water evaporates into the air as a gas and returns to Earth as rain or snow.

2.1 The Water Cycle

> **THINGS YOU WILL NEED:**
> - **an adult**
> - **safety goggles**
> - tin can
> - ice cubes
> - water
> - saucepan
> - stove
> - tongs

You can make a simple model of Earth's water cycle.

1. Remove labels from a tin can.
2. Half fill the can with ice cubes. Add water to the same level.
3. Add about an inch of water to a saucepan. **Ask an adult** to heat the water on a stove.
4. When the water is boiling, **put on safety goggles**. Then use tongs to hold the can of ice water about 15 cm (6 in) above the pan.
5. Look for water condensing, or changing from a gas to a liquid, on the cold can. Soon a few drops will become large enough to fall back into the pan. It is raining into the pan.

In the natural world, a similar process happens. Water evaporates and condenses to form clouds, which are made up of tiny water droplets. These droplets bump into one another and grow until gravity causes them to fall to the ground as raindrops.

2.2 **Measuring Raindrops**

THINGS YOU WILL NEED:

- rain
- cookie pan
- plastic wrap
- metric ruler
- magnifying glass
- calculator (optional)
- pen or pencil
- notebook
- deep pan
- fine flour
- eyedroppers

You can measure the size of raindrops. If rain consists of fine, gently falling drops, you can collect raindrops quite easily.

1. Cover a cookie pan with plastic wrap. Then take it out into the rain and collect a few drops on the plastic.

2. Take the pan inside. Work quickly before the drops evaporate. The drops, as you can see, are tiny hemispheres.

3. Place a metric ruler beside a drop and measure its diameter. If the drop is very small, observe both drop and ruler through a magnifying glass.

4. Measure and record the diameters of a dozen or more drops.

5. The volume of the drops can be calculated from the diameter of the hemispheres. Table 1 gives the volume for a number of different hemisphere diameters.

   What is the average volume of the raindrops you collected?

6. In heavier rain, let a few drops fall into a pan that contains at least 2.5 cm (1 in) of fine flour. Each drop will form a dough pellet. When the pellets are dry, measure their diameters with a ruler.

TABLE 1.

Volume of a Raindrop When the Diameter of Its Hemisphere Is Known

Diameter of hemisphere (mm)	Volume of drop (mm³)	Diameter of hemisphere (mm)	Volume of drop (mm³)
1	0.26	6	56.5
2	2.1	7	89.8
3	7.1	8	134
4	16.8	9	191
5	32.7	10	262

If you are thinking like a good scientist, you will say, "I doubt that the raindrops are the same size as the pellets." You are absolutely right! However, you can let drops of known size fall from an eyedropper into the flour and find the ratio between the diameters of liquid drops and flour pellets.

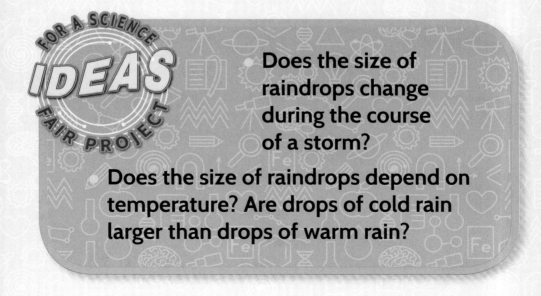

IDEAS FOR A SCIENCE FAIR PROJECT

- Does the size of raindrops change during the course of a storm?
- Does the size of raindrops depend on temperature? Are drops of cold rain larger than drops of warm rain?

2.3 Tiny Droplets Grow Larger

THINGS YOU WILL NEED:
- wax paper
- eyedropper
- toothpick
- penny

When moist (humid) air rises, it expands because air pressure is usually less at higher altitudes. Expanding gases cool. The colder water vapor may begin to condense on tiny particles such as salt and dust that are plentiful in the atmosphere. The drops are tiny. But as they collide with other drops, they grow. Eventually, they may become so heavy that they fall to the ground. This experiment will show you why tiny droplets may grow larger.

1. Spread a sheet of wax paper on a counter.

2. Using an eyedropper, place several small drops of water close together on the wax paper.

3. Use a toothpick to move one drop very close to another. What happens when they touch? What happens to the size of the drop?

4. Continue to bring other drops to the larger one you just made. What happens to the size of the drop?

   As you can see, water drops are attracted to one another. This cohesive property of water can be demonstrated in another way.

5. Use an eyedropper to add water drop by drop to the top of a penny. How many drops can you add? How high can you heap the water before it is overcome by gravity?

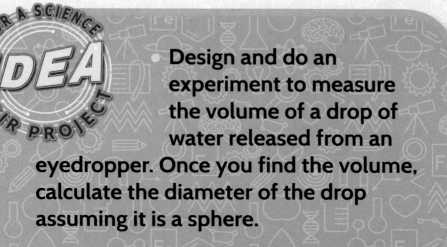

Design and do an experiment to measure the volume of a drop of water released from an eyedropper. Once you find the volume, calculate the diameter of the drop assuming it is a sphere.

2.4 Falling Raindrops

THINGS YOU WILL NEED:

- tall glass
- cooking oil
- eyedropper
- water
- vacuum cleaner that can blow air
- garage, basement, or day without wind
- Ping-Pong ball
- food coloring

Artists often draw tear-shaped raindrops. Are raindrops really tear shaped?

It is difficult to see what a raindrop looks like as it falls through the air. However, we can watch a drop as it falls slowly through a less dense liquid.

1. Nearly fill a tall glass with cooking oil.

2. Fill an eyedropper with water. Hold the eyedropper above the glass of cooking oil.

3. Squeeze a drop of water from the eyedropper. Watch the drop fall through the oil.

4. Repeat the experiment a few times to get a better sense of the falling drop's shape. What is its shape?

Some vacuum cleaners can blow air out as well as suck air into the machine. If you have such a machine, you can see the shape of raindrops in another way. To avoid staining household items, do this experiment in a garage, a basement, or outside on a calm day.

5. Arrange the vacuum so that it is blowing an upward stream of air. To locate the air stream, place a Ping-Pong ball where you feel the stream. What happens to the Ping-Pong ball?

6. Add a few drops of food coloring to a glass of water.

7. Use an eyedropper to place some colored drops in the air stream. Release the drops from different heights. You will find a place where the drops remain at rest or fall slowly. Look at the drops. What is their shape?

2.5 Terminal Velocity

THINGS YOU WILL NEED:

- coffee filter
- stopwatch
- meterstick or yardstick
- calculator (optional)
- pen or pencil
- notebook

Falling objects accelerate because the force of gravity pulls on them. A sky diver's speed increases by almost 10 m/s (33 ft/s) every second for the first several seconds. But very soon the speed becomes constant at about 200 km/hr (125 mi/hr, 55 m/s, or 182 ft/s). Friction between the air and the falling body creates an upward force that balances the force of gravity. The sky diver then falls at a constant speed, which is called terminal velocity. After the parachute opens, a slower terminal velocity allows for a safe landing.

1. To see what happens to a falling raindrop, let an open coffee filter represent a raindrop. Use a stopwatch to measure the time for the filter to fall to the floor from a height of 1 m (39 in). Repeat your measurements several times to be sure they are consistent.

2. Calculate and record the filter's average speed during its fall.

3. Measure and record the times to fall 0.5 m (1.6 ft), 1.5 m (5 ft), and 2 m (6.5 ft). You might try even greater heights if you have high ceilings.

4. For each height, find the average speed at which the coffee filter falls. Are all the speeds very nearly the same? If they are, what does that tell you about the time for the filter to reach its terminal velocity? Suppose all the speeds are not all the same. Can you figure out about how far or long the filter falls before reaching a terminal speed?

Place one coffee filter inside a second. Drop the two together. Does the terminal velocity double? Does it take longer to reach a terminal velocity? What happens to the speeds and terminal velocities if you drop three filters? Four filters?

Try to measure the terminal velocities of objects such as feathers, leaves, paper, dust particles, and other light objects as they fall through air.

Do an experiment to determine the acceleration of a falling object, such as a lead weight or a brick.

2.6 Snowflakes

THINGS YOU WILL NEED:

- dark construction paper or dark felt cloth
- cold, protected place outside
- snow
- thermometer
- magnifying glass
- pen or pencil
- notebook
- glass plates or glass microscope slides
- wood shingle or cardboard sheet
- spray can of clear lacquer or any clear polyvinyl spray
- microscope (optional)

You found a way to capture raindrops. You can also capture snow-flakes! You can even preserve them and take them inside where it is warm.

1. Find a sheet of dark construction paper or a dark felt cloth. Put it in a cold place outside where snow can't fall on it. An unheated garage, a shed, a porch, or another protected place will serve your purpose. The temperature must be below 0°C (32°F).

2. When it is snowing, collect a few flakes on the paper or cloth. Just let the flakes fall onto the paper or cloth. Examine them with a magnifying glass. Be careful not to breathe on the flakes. You might like to photograph or sketch a few of the flakes. They can be quite beautiful.

3. You can preserve snowflakes. Put a number of glass plates (glass microscope slides work well) on a wood shingle or cardboard sheet. Put them in a cold, protected place so the

temperature of the glass will become lower than 0°C (32°F). Put a spray can of clear lacquer in the same cold place.

4. When the glass and lacquer are cold, spray a thin layer of lacquer on each glass. Hold the can approximately 25 cm (10 in) above the glass.

5. Put on gloves. Then hold the shingle or cardboard sheet in the falling snow. Capture a number of snowflakes on the cold, wet lacquer.

6. Put the shingle or cardboard back in the cold, protected place. Leave it for several hours until the lacquer has dried.

7. Once the lacquer has dried, you can bring the glass slides or plates inside.

8. Examine the flakes with a magnifier or microscope. Do the flakes have a common shape? Are any two alike?

9. Collect and preserve snowflakes from several snowfalls. See if you can classify the snowflakes into the following kinds: plates, stellars (star-shaped), columns, capped columns, needles, irregular, and sleet.

Do the snowflakes from different snowstorms have distinctly different shapes?

Find a way to preserve frost patterns that form on cold glass.

Can you find a way to preserve snowflakes that are already on the ground?

2.7 Build a Rain Gauge

Weather stations keep a record of rainfall, which is measured in centimeters or inches. A centimeter of rain would cover the ground with water a centimeter deep. Of course, water usually seeps into the ground where it can add to wells or be absorbed by plants.

Weather stations have rain gauges that measure rainfall very accurately. One type has a bucket attached to a scale. As rain collects in the bucket, the weight on the scale moves a pen connected to the balance. The pen leaves a mark on a piece of paper that is fixed to a drum that turns slowly. By looking at the rising mark on the paper, meteorologists can see how much rain has fallen. Since the drum turns at a known speed, they can also determine the rate at which the rain is falling.

You can make a much simpler gauge to measure rain.

1. Find a tall, clear plastic vial or a tall, clear jar with straight sides, such as an olive jar.

2. Drive a stake into open ground away from trees or buildings. Fasten the vial or jar to the stake. Be sure the top of the vial or jar is higher than the top of the stake. See Figure 6a.

Figure 6. You can make rain gauges to measure rainfall.

3. After a rainstorm, use a ruler to measure the depth of water in the vial or jar. Record the amount of rain in centimeters or inches. Compare your measurements with those reported in your local newspaper or weather website. Don't be too concerned if they don't agree. Rainfall, particularly from showers, can vary a lot over even short distances.

4. Be sure to check the gauge every morning. Sometimes it rains at night when you are sleeping.

5. Here is another way to measure rainfall. Put a wide funnel in a tall, clean jar with straight sides. An olive jar or a large peanut butter jar works well. Rain that falls into the funnel will collect in the jar (Figure 6b).

6. Measure the depth of water in the jar. The funnel's mouth is wider than the jar. Therefore, the actual depth of the rainfall can be determined from this formula:

$$\text{Depth of rain} = \text{depth of water in jar} \times \frac{(\text{diameter of jar})^2}{(\text{diameter of funnel})^2}$$

Why are the diameters squared? See if you can explain why this formula works.

From your measurements, how much rain fell in your town during a period of one year? How do your measurements of annual rainfall compare with those reported by your local newspaper?

2.8 How Much Water Is in Snow?

THINGS YOU WILL NEED:

- ruler, yardstick, or meterstick
- shovel
- tall, empty coffee can
- snow
- ruler
- calculator (optional)

Sometimes precipitation falls as snow. When spring arrives in cold climates, water from melting snow flows into lakes and rivers. If there is an abundance of snow or if the snow melts too fast, cities, towns, and farms can be flooded. You can convert snow depths into depths of rain quite easily.

1. After a snowstorm, use a ruler or yardstick to measure the depth of the snow. Then shovel away the snow from an area of ground. You then have a place where you can measure the depth of the next snowstorm.

2. Find a tall coffee can. Fill it with loose snow. Do not pack it down.

3. Bring the can inside and let the snow melt. Use a ruler to measure the depth of the water in the can. Then measure the inside depth of the can. From the ratio depth of the can/depth of the water, you can calculate the rain that fell as snow. For example, suppose the can is 16 cm tall and the depth of the water is 2 cm. Then the ratio is 8:1. Every 8 cm of snow has the same amount of water as 1 cm of rain.

You will have to repeat this procedure for every snowfall. Dry, fluffy snow might require 25 cm (10 in) of snow to provide 1 cm (0.4 in) of rain. Five centimeters (2 in) of wet, slushy snow might be the equivalent of 1 cm of rain.

Chapter 3

Weather Instruments

Meteorologists use tools to study the weather. So far, you have experimented with some weather instruments, such as a barometer and a rain gauge. Are you ready to use some different weather instruments?

Every weather station has a thermometer. It is usually one that will read each day's high and low temperatures. There will be instruments to measure wind speed and direction. A hygrometer or sling psychrometer can be used to measure humidity. And dew points are measured daily.

With these instruments, you can have your own weather station and keep daily weather records. Study your records and the sky. You will find that you can begin to make predictions about tomorrow's weather. You may already have discovered that decreasing air pressure, as signaled by your barometer, indicates the possibility of rain. And you may have noticed that increasing air pressure usually precedes fair weather.

3.1 A Thermometer

THINGS YOU WILL NEED:

- eyedropper
- food coloring
- test tube or small bottle with a narrow mouth
- water
- clear plastic drinking straw or length of glass tubing
- modeling clay
- 2 coffee mugs
- clock or watch
- marking pen
- hot water
- cold water
- ruler

An experiment will help you to see how a thermometer works.

1. Add several drops of food coloring to a test tube or small bottle with a narrow mouth.

2. Completely fill the test tube or bottle with water.

3. Put one end of a clear drinking straw or a length of glass tubing in the water. Leave most of the straw or tubing above the mouth of the test tube or bottle.

4. Surround the straw and plug the mouth of the test tube or bottle with modeling clay. The clay should cover and fill the opening. It should fit snugly around the straw or glass tubing so that air cannot enter or leave the test tube or bottle.

5. Push the clay plug firmly into the mouth of the test tube or bottle. This should push colored water about halfway up the drinking straw as shown in Figure 7.

6. Put the test tube or bottle in a coffee mug. Leave it for ten minutes so the water can reach room temperature.

7. Use a marking pen to mark the water level on the straw or glass tubing.

clear straw or
glass tube

clay

colored water

cup

Figure 7. A simple thermometer.

8. Add hot water to the mug. What happens to the water level in the straw or tubing? Mark this new level.

9. Put the test tube or bottle in another mug that contains cold water. What happens to the water level in the straw or tubing? Mark this new level. What happens to the volume of water when it warms? When it cools?

10. Use a ruler and the marking pen to divide the spaces between your two marks into equal degrees. You have made a simple thermometer with a temperature scale.

Temperature Scales

Scientists use a thermometer scale that was invented in 1742 by Anders Celsius (1701–1744), a Swedish astronomer. Another temperature scale widely used in the United States was invented in 1714 by Gabriel Daniel Fahrenheit (1686–1736), a German scientist. Both scientists used mercury, a liquid metal, in their sealed thermometers. Mercury remains a liquid over a wide range of temperatures. Mercury also expands and contracts by even amounts with changes in temperature. **Because mercury is poisonous, you should not use mercury thermometers.** Use alcohol or digital thermometers instead.

Today, both temperature scales are based on two fixed temperatures—the boiling and freezing temperatures of water at an air pressure of 76 cm of mercury. On the Celsius scale, water freezes at 0° and boils at 100°. On the Fahrenheit scale, water freezes at 32° and boils at 212°. This book gives temperatures in both degrees Celsius (°C) and Fahrenheit (°F). Of course, the temperature at which water boils or freezes at sea level pressure doesn't change. The two scales simply assign different numbers to these fixed temperatures. You could invent your own scale and assign still different numbers to the fixed points. For example, you could assign 0° to the freezing point of water and 50° to the boiling point. Then one degree on your scale would equal two degrees on the Celsius scale.

IDEAS FOR A SCIENCE FAIR PROJECT

- Investigate why the Fahrenheit scale has such strange numbers (32 and 212) for its fixed points.

- Obtain a thermometer that has no scale. You may be able to borrow one from your school or buy one from one of the science supply companies found in the appendix. **Under adult supervision**, devise a scale for the thermometer. You might use one of the two common scales or invent one of your own.

- Make a thermometer that uses air rather than a liquid to measure temperature.

3.2 Graphing the Temperature

THINGS YOU WILL NEED:

- outdoor thermometer, preferably one that can measure daily high and low temperatures
- notebook
- pen or pencil
- sunny days
- clock or watch
- graph paper

1. Obtain an outdoor thermometer. If possible, get a thermometer that can measure daily high and low temperatures.

2. Outside temperatures should be measured in the shade. Hang the thermometer in a place that is always shaded.

3. Using your thermometer, record daily high and low temperatures. After a year, examine your records. Which month was the coldest? The warmest?

   What is the warmest time on a sunny day? You might think it is in the middle of the day. That is when the sun feels warmest. But is it?

4. To find the warmest time of day, use your outdoor thermometer. Record the temperature every hour from 8 a.m. until 6 or 7 p.m. Do this for several sunny days. Do it during different seasons of the year.

5. Make a graph of your results. Plot temperature on the vertical axis versus time on the horizontal axis. Compare your results with the sample results in Figure 8.

   How can you explain your results? The sample results?

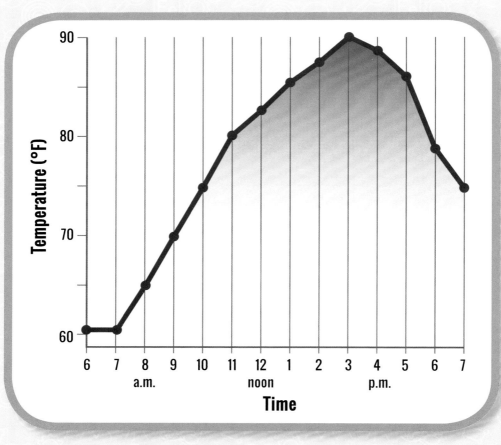

Figure 8. A graph shows outdoor temperatures from sunrise to sunset on a late summer day.

IDEAS FOR A SCIENCE FAIR PROJECT

- Design and do experiments to see how clouds affect air temperature.
- Do clouds at night affect temperature in the same way as daytime clouds?

3.3 A Look at Wind

THINGS YOU WILL NEED:

- **an adult**
- balloon
- saw
- soft wood, such as pine, approximately 1.3 c m (0.5 in) thick
- heavy-duty aluminum pie or baking pans
- shears
- ruler
- hacksaw
- glue
- drill and bit
- nail
- tall post
- plastic washer
- hammer
- long plastic bag
- tape or tacks
- small stones

Wind, particularly changes in wind direction, can be a key to predicting the weather. To find the direction of the wind, you can build a wind vane, often called a weather vane.

1. **Ask an adult** to cut a piece of soft wood approximately 30 cm (12 in) long, 2.5 cm (1 in) wide, and 1.3 cm (0.5 in) thick.

2. The vane can be an arrow. The arrow's head and tail can be cut from heavy-duty aluminum pie or baking pans using shears. Make the tail a trapezoid about 8 cm (3 in) wide, 18 cm (7 in) long on one side, and 10 cm (4 in) long on the other side. The head of the arrow can be a triangle with a base of 7.5 cm (3 in) and an altitude of the same length.

3. **Ask an adult** to use a hacksaw to cut a vertical slit at each end of the stick. Slide the head and tail of the weather vane arrow into these slits. Then glue them in place (Figure 9).

49

4. Balance the arrow on your finger. **Ask an adult** to drill a hole through the shaft at the balancing point. The hole should be slightly wider than the diameter of the nail you will use to fasten the weather vane to a post. The post should be as tall as possible. It should be in an open area far from buildings and trees.

5. Place a plastic washer between the vane and the post to which it will be nailed.

6. Use a nail to attach the weather vane to the post. Put the nail through the hole drilled through the shaft and then the washer. Then hammer the nail into the post. Leave a space between the nail head and the vane so that the vane can turn freely.

7. Cut a long plastic bag into strips. Tape or tack one end of the strips to the upper part of the post. The plastic strips can serve as a

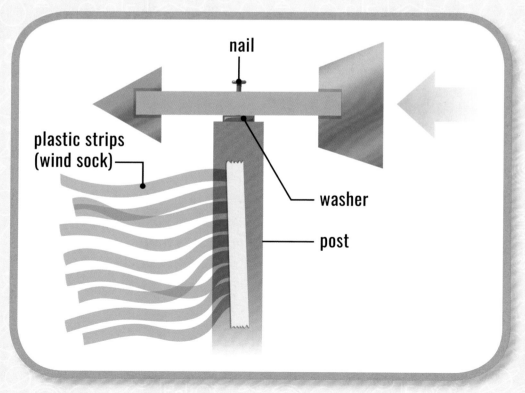

Figure 9. You can make a weather vane and a wind sock and attach them to a post.

wind sock like the kind seen at small airports. The wind sock will also help you find wind directions. Your wind sock may detect the direction of winds too light to turn the vane.

Bear in mind that wind direction is the direction from which the wind is blowing. If you feel a wind against your face when facing north, it is a north wind. If you don't know directions at the site of the post, you can easily find north. In the United States and Canada, the shortest shadow cast by the post will point north.

8. As the sun approaches its midpoint in the sky, start marking the end of the post's shadow every few minutes. You can use small stones to do this. Do this until you are sure the shadow is growing longer. The end of the shortest shadow will point toward the North Pole. Knowing north, you can identify all the other directions. Face north. South will be behind you. Raise both arms. Your right hand will point east; your left hand points west.

9. Keep daily records of wind direction. Pay particular attention to changes in the wind's direction. See if these changes in wind direction can help you predict changes in the weather.

IDEAS FOR A SCIENCE FAIR PROJECT

- Does midday always occur at the same time? Use a stick's shortest shadow to find out.

- At the site of your wind vane, does a compass needle point toward north? If not, why doesn't it?

3.4 Wind Speed

> **THINGS YOU WILL NEED:**
> - anemometer (optional)
> - Beaufort scale (Table 2)

Meteorologists use an anemometer to measure wind speed. Anemometers have three cups that rotate when the wind blows. The anemometer's spinning shaft turns a small generator. The generator produces an electric current that turns a needle on a meter dial. The faster the wind, the greater the current and the more the needle turns.

1. If you have an anemometer, you can use it to measure wind speeds.
2. If you don't have an anemometer, you can use the Beaufort scale to estimate wind speeds. The scale was devised by Sir Francis Beaufort (1774–1857), a hydrographer in the British Navy. Using the Beaufort scale (Table 2), you can estimate wind speeds by observing things moved by the wind.

Humidity

Air always contains some water molecules. Dry air holds relatively few water molecules. Damp or humid air contains lots of water molecules. Table 3 shows the mass of water vapor per cubic meter of air needed to saturate, or fill to capacity, air at different temperatures. As you can see, it takes more water to saturate warm air than to saturate cold air. You can find the mass of water needed to saturate a cubic meter of air at temperatures not given in the table. Simply plot a graph of air temperature versus the mass of water vapor using the information in Table 3. Draw the best curve connecting the points you plot. Use the graph to find any value of water vapor per cubic meter saturated from 0°C to 35°C (32°F to 95°F).

TABLE 2.
The Beaufort Scale

Beaufort Number	Wind	Wind Speed		Visual Observations
		(mph)	(kph)	
0	calm	0	0	Smoke rises vertically.
1	light air	1-3	2-5	Wind direction given by smoke but not by wind vane.
2	light breeze	4-7	6-12	Leaves rustle; wind vane moves; can feel wind on your face.
3	gentle breeze	8-12	13-19	Wind extends small flags; leaves in constant motion.
4	moderate breeze	13-18	20-29	Small branches move; dust and loose paper lifted.
5	fresh breeze	19-24	30-38	Small trees with leaves sway; wavelets form on lakes.
6	strong breeze	25-31	39-50	Large branches moving; utility lines seem to whistle.
7	near gale	32-38	51-61	Whole trees moving; some difficulty walking into wind.
8	gale	39-46	62-74	Twigs break off trees; difficult to walk against wind.
9	strong gale	47-54	75-86	Slight damage to buildings.
10	storm	55-63	87-101	Trees uprooted; considerable damage to buildings.
11	violent storm	64-74	102-118	Widespread damage.
12	hurricane	75+	119+	Extreme destruction of property.

Absolute humidity is the actual mass of water vapor in a cubic meter of air. It can be determined by measuring the dew point. You will see how that is done in the next experiment.

Relative humidity, usually expressed as a percent, is the mass of water vapor in a cubic meter of air compared with the amount it would hold if it were saturated with water vapor. For example, if 1 m³ of air at 30°C (86°F) contains 15 g of water vapor, the relative humidity is 50 percent. Saturated air at 30°C would contain 30 g/m³. Since the air holds only 15 g, it contains half (50 percent) of the vapor needed to saturate that air.

High humidity can lead to rain. A hot, humid day in summer is often followed by a thunderstorm. As the warm, moist air rises, it cools. The vapor condenses into droplets, forming clouds. The clouds may grow until they become very large and anvil-shaped. The droplets may grow until they are large enough to overcome updrafts (upward moving air). Then they fall, sometimes accompanied by lightning and thunder. Thunder is the result of expanding air heated by lightning.

TABLE 3.

Maximum Mass of Water Vapor in a Cubic Meter of Air at Different Temperatures

Air Temperature		Mass of water vapor in a cubic meter of saturated air (g/m³)
°C	°F	
0	32	4.8
5	41	6.8
10	50	9.3
15	59	12.7
20	68	17.1
25	77	22.8
30	86	30.0
35	95	39.2

3.5 Relative Humidity

THINGS YOU WILL NEED:

- **an adult**
- sling psychrometer (optional)
- 2 identical thermometers
- thin board
- duct tape
- drill and bit
- length of thin rope
- cotton gauze
- rubber band
- water
- notebook
- pen or pencil
- Table 4a or Table 4b

If you have a sling psychrometer, you can use it to measure relative humidity. If not, you can make one. See Figure 10.

1. Find two identical thermometers and a thin board. The board should be wide enough so that both thermometers can be taped to the board.

2. The bulb of one thermometer should extend beyond one end of the board. It will be the wet-bulb thermometer. Cover that bulb with cotton gauze. Use a rubber band to hold the gauze in place. The other thermometer will be the dry-bulb thermometer.

3. **Have an adult** drill a hole near one end of the board. Slip a length of thin rope through the hole. Tie the rope to make a loop that can serve as the handle of your sling psychrometer.

4. Wet the gauze with water at room temperature. Then swing the board in the air for a minute or more. The wet-bulb thermometer will show a decrease in temperature. Continue swinging until there is no further decrease in the temperature of the wet-bulb thermometer.

5. Record the temperatures of both the wet-bulb and dry-bulb thermometers.

6. Find the temperature difference. Subtract the wet-bulb temperature from the dry-bulb temperature.

7. Use Table 4a or Table 4b (depending on whether you are measuring in Fahrenheit or Celsius) to find the relative humidity. First find the temperature closest to the dry-bulb temperature on the left side of the table. Next find the number at the top of the table that matches the difference between the dry- and wet-bulb temperatures.

   The relative humidity, as a percent, is where the dry-bulb temperature row intersects the temperature difference column. For example, if the dry-bulb temperature is 20°C and the wet-bulb temperature is 15°C, then the humidity is 58 percent.

Table 4a: Finding Relative Humidity (Percent) Using Fahrenheit Temperatures																					
Difference in Temperature (dry-bulb temp — wet-bulb temp)																						
Dry-Bulb Temp	1	2	3	4	5	6	7	8	9	10	11	12	13	14	15	16	17	16	19	20	25	30
0	67	33																				
5	73	46	20																			
10	78	56	34	13																		
15	82	64	46	29	11																	
20	85	70	55	40	26	12																
25	87	74	62	49	37	25	13															
30	89	78	67	56	46	36	26	16														
35	91	81	72	63	54	45	36	27	19	10												
40	92	83	75	68	60	52	45	37	29	22	15											
45	93	86	78	71	64	57	51	44	38	31	25	18	12									
50	93	87	80	74	67	61	55	49	43	38	32	27	21	16	10							
55	94	88	82	76	70	65	59	54	49	43	38	33	28	23	19	14						
60	94	89	83	78	73	68	63	58	53	48	43	39	34	30	26	21	17	13				
65	95	90	85	80	75	70	66	61	56	52	48	44	39	35	31	27	24	20	16	12		
70	95	90	86	81	77	72	68	64	59	55	51	48	44	40	36	33	29	25	22	19		
75	96	91	86	82	78	74	70	66	62	58	54	51	47	44	40	37	34	30	27	24		
80	96	91	87	83	79	75	72	68	64	61	57	54	50	47	44	41	38	35	32	29	15	
85	96	92	88	84	80	76	73	69	66	62	59	56	52	49	46	43	41	38	35	32	20	
90	96	92	89	85	81	78	74	71	68	65	61	58	55	52	49	47	44	41	39	36	24	
95	96	93	89	85	82	79	75	72	69	66	63	60	57	54	51	49	46	43	41	38	27	
100	96	93	89	86	83	80	77	73	70	68	65	62	59	56	54	51	49	46	44	41	30	21

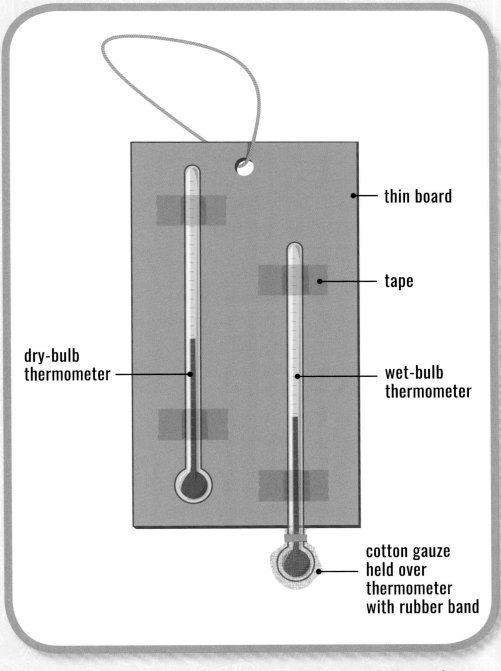

thin board

tape

dry-bulb thermometer

wet-bulb thermometer

cotton gauze held over thermometer with rubber band

Figure 10. You can build a sling psychrometer to measure relative humidity.

Table 4b: Finding Relative Humidity (Percent) Using Celsius Temperatures															
Difference in Temperature (dry-bulb temp—wet-bulb temp)															
Dry-Bulb Temp	0.5	1.0	1.5	2.0	2.5	3.0	3.5	4.0	4.5	5.0	7.5	10.0	12.5	15.0	17.5	20.0
–15	79	79	58	38	18											
–12.5	82	65	47	30	13											
–10	85	69	54	39	24	10										
–7.5	87	73	60	48	35	22	10									
–5	88	77	66	54	43	32	21	11								
–2.5	90	80	70	60	50	42	37	22	12							
0	91	82	73	65	56	47	39	31	23	15						
2.5	92	84	76	68	61	53	46	38	31	24						
5	93	86	78	71	65	58	51	45	38	32						
7.5	93	87	80	74	68	62	56	50	44	38						
10	94	88	82	76	71	65	60	54	49	44	19					
12.5	94	89	84	78	73	68	63	58	53	48	25					
15	95	90	85	80	75	70	66	61	57	52	31	12				
17.5	95	90	86	81	77	72	68	64	60	55	36	18				
20	95	91	87	82	78	74	70	66	62	58	40	24				
22.5	96	92	87	83	80	76	72	68	64	61	44	28	14			
25	96	92	88	84	81	77	73	70	66	63	47	32	19			
27.5	96	92	89	85	82	78	75	71	68	65	50	36	23	12		
30	96	93	89	86	82	79	76	73	70	67	52	39	27	16		
32.5	97	93	90	86	83	80	77	74	71	68	54	42	30	20	11	
35	97	93	90	87	84	81	78	75	72	69	56	44	33	23	14	
37.5	97	94	91	87	85	82	79	76	73	70	58	46	36	26	18	10
40	97	94	91	88	85	82	79	77	74	72	59	48	38	29	21	13

3.6 Dew Points and Absolute Humidity

THINGS YOU WILL NEED:

- shiny metal can
- warm water
- thermometer
- ice
- notebook
- pen or pencil
- Table 3
- sling psychrometer you made in Experiment 3.5

You have probably seen moisture condense on a glass of cold lemonade or soda. A similar thing often happens outside on a cool night. Dew forms on blades of grass or other surfaces. Water vapor in the air condenses on cool surfaces. This happens when the temperature of the air falls to a temperature at which it is saturated with water vapor. For example, suppose 20°C (68°F) air at sunset contains 12.7 g/m³ of water vapor. If at midnight the air temperature has fallen to 15°C (59°F), moisture will begin to condense. The air at 15°C (59°F) will be saturated. Look back at Table 3.

The temperature at which air becomes saturated with moisture and begins to condense is called the dew point. Using the dew point and Table 3, you can determine the absolute and relative humidity of the air.

In mild weather, you can find the dew point of air quite easily. It is more difficult to do in cold weather.

1. Fill a shiny metal can about two-thirds full with warm water. Insert a thermometer and stir.

2. Add a small piece of ice and continue to stir. Watch the surface of the can.

3. Continue adding small pieces of ice and stirring until you see moisture forming on the can. When you see moisture, immediately read the thermometer. That temperature is the dew point.

4. Use the dew point and Table 3 to find the absolute humidity of the air in grams per cubic meter.

5. Use the same information to find the relative humidity.

6. Find the relative humidity using your sling psychrometer. How does it compare with the relative humidity you found in step 5? Which do you think is more accurate? Why?

IDEAS FOR A SCIENCE FAIR PROJECT

- **Is the humidity inside a building the same as the humidity outside? Do experiments to find out.**

- **Which season of the year is the most humid where you live? Do experiments to find out.**

- **Design and do an experiment to find the frost point, or the temperature at which frost forms.**

Dew Points and Weather

Dew points can tell you a lot about weather. An increasing dew point indicates a growing amount of moisture in the air and a possibility of rain. A decreasing dew point indicates that the air is drying and leading to fair weather.

In the summer, dew points can be useful in predicting comfort levels. Dew points exceeding 21°C (70°F) indicate air that will feel oppressive to many people. Dew points from 16 to 21°C (60 to 70°F) will cause many people to feel uncomfortable, even when air temperatures are the same.

Chapter 4

Wind and Sky

As you have seen, using tools like a thermometer, barometer, and rain gauge can help you learn about and predict weather. Can you also look at the sky to learn more about weather? The sky can actually provide some beautiful sights—sunsets, sunrises, halos, Northern Lights, full moons, lunar eclipses, and much more. However, never look directly at the sun. It can damage your eyes.

Lie on the grass and look up at puffy, white cumulus clouds. It can be a pleasant way to spend time. With a little imagination, you will see all kinds of things—animals, people, buildings, and interesting shapes. But cloud cover, or the fraction of the sky covered, and the types of cloud should also be part of your daily weather records.

Cloud Types

There are three main types of clouds: cirrus, cumulus, and stratus. Cirrus clouds are the highest. They form more than 7 km (4.3 mi) above Earth's surface. At such altitudes, the air is very cold. As a result, cirrus clouds consist of tiny ice crystals. Cirrus clouds have a thin, wispy appearance. They are often blown by the wind into feathery strands called mare's tails. Sunlight, either from the sun or reflected from the moon, can form a rainbow-colored ring or halo when it passes through cirrus clouds. A ring around the moon often indicates that rain will follow.

Cumulus clouds are white, puffy, fair-weather clouds. They are commonly seen on warm summer days. On warm, humid days, they sometimes grow into huge cumulonimbus clouds that lead to thunderstorms. (*Nimbus* is the Latin word for rain cloud.)

Stratus clouds are close to Earth's surface. They usually cover the entire sky and often bring rain or snow.

Meteorologists have additional names for clouds. They use three prefixes to classify clouds according to height. The prefix *cirro-* means clouds at altitudes higher than 6.1 km (3.8 mi). *Alto-* applies to clouds at middle altitudes of 2 to 6 km (1.2 to 3.8mi). *Strato-* means low-altitude clouds, from ground level (fog) to 2 km (1.2 mi).

Using these prefixes, a variety of additional clouds are named: cirrostratus, cirrocumulus, altostratus, altocumulus, nimbostratus, stratocumulus, and cumulonimbus. How would you describe each of these clouds?

Record any clouds you see in your daily weather records. You will find that clouds can often help you predict tomorrow's weather. For example, an approaching cold air mass may force warm air in front of it to move upward. As the warm air expands at higher altitudes, its moisture may condense, giving rise to high cirrus clouds. These clouds may thicken into cirrostratus and other stratus clouds to produce rain or snow.

4.1 Can You Make a Cloud?

THINGS YOU WILL NEED:

- **an adult**
- clear, empty, 2-liter plastic soda bottle with screw-on cap
- warm water
- light background, such as a window
- matches
- freezer

You may have made a cloud accidentally by opening a cold soda on a hot day. The cloud probably appeared briefly just above the opening.

A cloud is really a huge collection of tiny raindrops. To see what factors are needed for clouds to form, you can do several experiments.

1. Find a clear, empty, 2- liter plastic soda bottle. Remove any labels that may be on it.
2. Pour about half a cup of warm water into the bottle.
3. Screw on the cap. Then shake the bottle to saturate the air inside with water vapor.
4. Hold the bottle up against a light background, such as a window.
5. Shake the bottle again. Then squeeze and release it to quickly reduce air pressure in the bottle. You will probably not see a cloud. Something must be missing.
6. **Ask an adult** to light a match, blow it out, and quickly drop it into the bottle. Put the cap back on. Smoke particles are now in the bottle.
7. Shake the bottle again and hold it up against a light back-ground. Squeeze it to increase the pressure inside the bottle.

Then suddenly release your squeeze. The pressure inside the bottle will decrease quickly. This allows the air and water vapor to expand. Did you see a cloud form?

The tiny smoke particles provided what are called condensation nuclei. These particles provide places on which water vapor can condense to form tiny droplets.

8. On a warm, humid day, you can make a cloud by opening the door to a freezer. The water vapor in the air will condense into tiny droplets when it meets the cold air in the freezer.

IDEAS FOR A SCIENCE FAIR PROJECT

• Design an experiment to see if a ring around the moon is a good indicator that precipitation will follow.

• To see the source of the salt particles, stand on an ocean beach at night. Shine a flashlight with a strong beam upward into the air. You will see reflected light from the salt particles and droplets. Design an experiment to find out where the salt particles come from.

4.2 Can You Make Fog?

> ### THINGS YOU WILL NEED:
> - wide-mouth jar
> - hot water
> - ice cube
> - window and daylight

Fog is simply a cloud at ground level. Fog forms when warm, humid air moves over a cold surface. Droplets of fog are very small—2 to 50 microns. (A micron is a millionth of a meter.) Nevertheless, they are more dense than air and fall slowly to the ground. They are quickly replaced by other droplets that condense on nuclei. You can see fog form in your kitchen.

1. Fill a wide-mouth jar with hot water. Pour out all but about 3 cm (1 in) of the water.

2. Carefully balance an ice cube on the edge of the jar.

3. Hold the jar up to the light. Look for thin streams of fog forming where warm, moist air meets the cold ice.

4. On a cold but humid day, watch what happens to your exhaled breath. Can you see fog forming in front of you?

4.3 Temperature Effects on Air

THINGS YOU WILL NEED:
- soap bubble solution
- plastic cover, such as one from a coffee can
- empty soda can
- pan
- hot water
- cotton ball
- rubbing alcohol

What happens to air when it is warmed or cooled? You can do an experiment to find out.

1. Pour some soap bubble solution into a plastic cover.

2. Remove the tab from an empty soda can.

3. Put the open end of the soda can in the bubble solution. Then stand the can upright. You should see a soap bubble over the opening in the can. The bubble seals the air in the can. No air can enter or leave until the bubble breaks.

4. Hold the can in your warm hands, but do not squeeze the can. What happens to the size of the bubble? Why?

5. Nearly fill a pan with hot water.

6. Repeat the experiment, but this time hold the can in the hot water. What happens to the size of the bubble? How is the volume of a gas affected by an increase in temperature? How will it affect the density of a gas? (Density is the mass of a gas divided by its volume.) Suppose the volume of a gas increases and the mass is unchanged. What happens to the gas's density?

7. Saturate a cotton ball with rubbing alcohol.

8. Repeat the experiment, but this time wipe the surface of the can with alcohol. What happens to the size of the bubble? What did the alcohol do to the temperature of the air in the can? How does a decrease in temperature affect the volume of a gas? How will it affect the density of a gas?

4.4 Density Effects on the Atmosphere

THINGS YOU WILL NEED:

- 2 clear vials or small glasses
- cold water
- hot water
- a dark food coloring
- eyedropper

As you saw in the previous experiment, a gas's density decreases when the gas's temperature increases. To see what happens when a warm air mass meets a cold air mass, we can use water as a model. Fluids are anything that can flow. Water and air are both fluids. They have many common properties, including how density affects them.

1. Fill a clear vial or small glass with cold water.

2. Fill a second clear vial or glass with hot water. Add a few drops of a dark food coloring to the hot water and stir.

3. Use an eyedropper to remove some of the colored hot water.

4. Place the end of the eyedropper near the bottom of the vial of cold water. Slowly squeeze the colored hot water into the cold water as shown in Figure 11. What happens to the warm water? What would happen to a warm (less dense) air mass if it overtook a colder (more dense) air mass?

5. Repeat the experiment, but this time color the cold water. The hot water should be clear.

6. Remove some of the colored cold water with an eyedropper.

7. Place the end of the eyedropper near the middle of the vial of hot water. Slowly squeeze the colored cold water into the hot water. What happens to the cold water? What do you think happens when a cold (more dense) air mass overtakes a warmer (less dense) air mass?

cold water

warm, colored water

Figure 11. How does the density of warm water compare with the density of cold water?

4.5 Sun and the Seasons

THINGS YOU WILL NEED:
- local daily newspaper
- notebook
- graph paper
- pen or pencil

Unless you live in a tropical location, you have seasons. Winters (from about December 21 to March 21) in the Northern Hemisphere are colder than summers (from about June 21 to September 21). To see how the hours of sunlight affect daily temperatures, you can collect data and plot graphs.

1. Examine the weather section in your daily newspaper. It probably contains the time at which the sun rises and sets. It may also include hours of sun or daylight. If not, you can figure it out. For example, if sunrise is at 6:30 a.m. and sunset is at 6:45 p.m., then that day has 12.25 hours of sunlight. In your notebook, record hours of sun each day or on one day each week for an entire year.

2. The same section may also give the official high and low temperatures for the previous day. With a thermometer that gives maximum and minimum temperatures, you could collect that information yourself. In your notebook, record maximum and minimum temperatures each day or on one day each week for an entire year.

3. On a long sheet of graph paper (you may need to tape several sheets together), plot graphs of the data you collected. For both graphs, plot days as sequential dates (1/1, 1/2, ... 12/30, 12/31) on the horizontal axis. On one graph, plot hours of sun on the vertical axis. On the other graph, plot the day's average temperature on the vertical axis.

4. According to your graphs, how does length of day affect average daily temperatures? What is the coldest month?

The warmest month? What month has the shortest days? The longest days? In what months, if any, might you expect to have snow?

- Design and do an experiment to map the sun's path across the sky during different seasons. When is the path longest? Shortest? Are your results what you would expect from Experiment 4.5?

- Design and do an experiment to measure the length of a vertical stick's midday shadow during different seasons. (Midday may not be at noon. Use time of sunrise and sunset to determine midday.) When is the shadow longest? Shortest? Are your results what you would expect from Experiment 4.5? Use the lengths of the stick and its shadow to find the sun's midday altitude.

- Investigate why setting and rising suns are often red. Then design a way to demonstrate this effect using a lightbulb to represent the sun.

4.6 A Look at Rainbows

THINGS YOU WILL NEED:

- watering hose with a spray nozzle
- bright sunshine
- pan
- water
- mirror
- tape
- white paper
- cardboard

Rainbows appear when drops of rain, fog, or dew are bathed in sunlight. The light rays reflected by the water drops are also refracted or bent as they enter and leave the water (Figure 12). Because the different colors in white light (violet to red) are refracted by different amounts, a spectrum or rainbow of colors can be seen. You can make rainbows by taking these properties of light and water into account.

1. Use the nozzle of a watering hose to spray a fine mist into the air on a sunny day. Stand with your back to the sun. Spray the water upward in front of you. You should see a rainbow reflected from the tiny water droplets. Which color is at the top of the rainbow? Which color is at the bottom?

2. You can also make a bright partial rainbow. Use a mirror to reflect light refracted by water. Place a pan of water in bright sunlight. Put a mirror in the water at an angle as shown in Figure 13.

3. Tape a sheet of white paper to a piece of cardboard to make a screen. Move the screen a meter (yard) or so above and in front of the mirror. Search for and find a bright portion of rainbow on the screen. Which color is on top? Which color is on the bottom? Are they in the same order that you saw them when you sprayed water into the air?

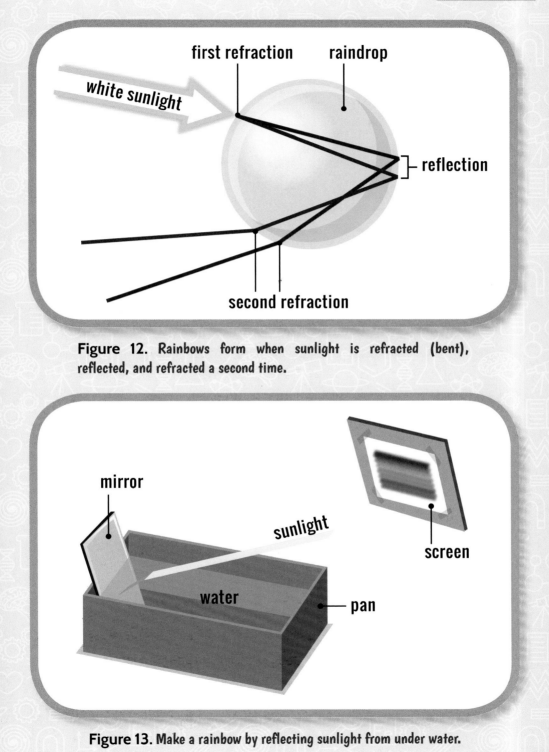

first refraction   raindrop

white sunlight

reflection

second refraction

Figure 12. Rainbows form when sunlight is refracted (bent), reflected, and refracted a second time.

mirror

sunlight

screen

water

pan

Figure 13. Make a rainbow by reflecting sunlight from under water.

Benjamin Franklin and a Storm

Like many early Americans, Benjamin Franklin (1706–1790) kept weather records. We associate Franklin with his famous (and very dangerous) kite experiment. That experiment demonstrated that clouds are electrically charged.

Franklin, who also invented bifocal eyeglasses and a more efficient stove, did much to improve our understanding of weather. He asked ship captains to measure water temperatures during their voyages. Their records led him to discover the warm current that flows northeastward from the Gulf of Mexico, called the Gulf Stream. This discovery explained, in part, why parts of Europe and Scandinavia enjoy a warmer climate than other areas at about the same latitude.

It was also Franklin who discovered that storms rotate counterclockwise about low pressure. In 1743, he was living in Philadelphia. One evening, he prepared to observe an eclipse of the moon. But a storm with northeast winds covered the sky, blocking any view of the moon. Later he discovered that people in Boston had observed the eclipse several hours before a similar storm struck that city. It seemed that the storm, despite its wind direction, had traveled from south to north.

Franklin was surprised. He had assumed that because the storm had northeast winds, it came from the northeast. Were that true, it should have reached Boston before Philadelphia. This led him to gather weather reports in newspapers from cities to his south and west. By tracking the path of storms that reached Philadelphia, he realized that nor'easters originated in the Gulf of Mexico and traveled northeastward. With a barometer and wind vane, he showed that storms are associated with low air pressure and counterclockwise winds.

The Telegraph and Nationwide Weather Stations

Nearly a century later, Joseph Henry (1797–1878) developed the basic mechanism for the telegraph in 1831. By 1835, Henry had invented the relay. This device allowed electric currents to be sent long distances by wire. Samuel F. B. Morse (1791–1872) is usually credited with the invention of the telegraph, but it was Henry who showed Morse how to build a telegraph. What Morse did was persuade Congress to fund a forty-mile telegraph line from Washington, DC, to Baltimore. And it was Morse who devised the dot-dash system of sending messages. The line was completed in 1844 and was a great success.

Soon after, telegraph lines connected all major American cities. This made it possible to collect weather information from all parts of the country. In 1849, Joseph Henry, then director of the Smithsonian Institution, established a network of weather stations. The stations were manned by volunteer observers. The data collected at these stations were telegraphed to Henry's office in Washington. There the data were used to draw weather maps and make the country's first weather predictions. Henry's network became known as the Weather Bureau. In 1870, Congress created what became the National Weather Service as part of the U.S. Army's Signal Corps. Later it became part of the Department of Agriculture. Still later it was moved to the Department of Commerce, where it remains today under the National Oceanic and Atmospheric Administration (NOAA).

Weather Maps

The National Weather Service gathers data from hundreds of weather stations around the world. That information is relayed to Washington, DC, by a set of symbols like the report shown in Figure 14a. In addition, stations launch helium or hydrogen balloons that collect data to a height of 30 km (19 mi). This information includes temperatures, air pressures, wind speeds and directions, humidity, and other weather indicators. The information is sent back to Earth by radio signals. More data are provided by weather satellites in orbits around Earth. These satellites provide periodic photos of Earth's entire surface so that storms can be tracked as they move.

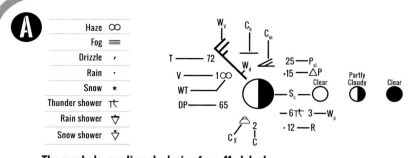

A

Haze	∞
Fog	≡
Drizzle	'
Rain	·
Snow	∗
Thunder shower	⇟
Rain shower	▽
Snow shower	▽

The symbols, reading clockwise from 11 o'clock:

Wv = wind velocity in knots (1 knot = 1.15 mph), full barb = 10 knot

Wd = wind direction (Wv symbols are tail of arrow)

Ch = type of high clouds

Cm = type of middle height clouds

Psi = air pressure in millibars at sea level

△P = change in air pressure over previous three hours

Sc = sky cover

Wp = weather over past six hours and the time it ended or started (three hours ago)

R = precipitation in last six hours, inches

C = ceiling (cloud height of lowest clouds)

Cl = low cloud type

Dp = dew point (°F)

WT = type of weather

V = visibility (mi)

T = temperature (°F)

B

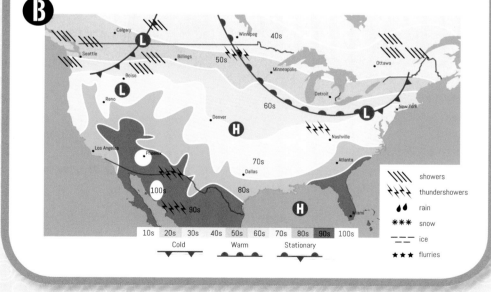

Figure 14. a) Weather data is shown after it is collected from a weather station. **b)** This weather map is similar to those found in newspapers.

The complex mass of data is analyzed by computers to prepare a national weather map. The map contains isobars (equal pressure lines) and isotherms (equal temperature lines) for North America. The map shows the positions of weather fronts, or places where large air masses meet. It also shows centers of high and low air pressure.

You can obtain less detailed weather maps from your local newspaper and TV station. These maps (Figure 14b) often use different colors to show isothermal areas. Hatched lines may be used to show where precipitation can be expected. The map in Figure 14b shows the symbols for fronts. A cold front is where a colder air mass has overtaken a warmer air mass. The reverse is true of a warm front. If the warm and cold air masses are not moving, their boundary is a stationary front.

Weather maps also show the centers of high and low pressure. These are indicated by the capital letters H or L. In the Northern Hemisphere, winds circulate clockwise about high pressure. They move counterclockwise about low pressure.

4.7 **Reading a Weather Map**

THINGS YOU WILL NEED:

- local newspaper's weather maps
- map of the United States or North America with a scale

1. Look at the weather section of your local daily newspaper. There you will probably find a weather map similar to the one in Figure 14b.
2. On the map, locate high and low pressure centers.
3. Locate warm, cold, and possibly stationary fronts.
4. Identify areas where precipitation can be expected.
5. What major city has the highest temperature? The lowest temperature?
6. Save these daily weather maps. Study the maps from one Monday to the next. In which general direction do air masses move across the United States? How about high and low pressure centers?
7. Determine the approximate average speed at which a front, a high, or a low is moving across the country. Do this by using the weather maps and a scaled map of the United States or North America.
8. Where on a weather map would you look to predict tomorrow's weather?

4.8 The Sun Heats Earth

THINGS YOU WILL NEED:

- construction paper
- paper clips
- several thermometers
- sheet of cardboard
- notebook
- pen or pencil
- clock or watch
- sunny day

The sun is Earth's heat source. An experiment will show you that this is true. An experiment can also show how color affects the rate of heating.

1. Prepare equal size sheets (5 cm by 10 cm or 2 in by 4 in) of different colors from construction paper. Be sure to include black and white as well as several bright colors.

2. Fold the paper sheets as shown in Figure 15. Put them over different thermometer bulbs. Hold them in place with paper clips as shown. (You will have to repeat the experiment several times if you have only one or two thermometers.)

3. Place the thermometers side by side on a sheet of cardboard. Record the temperature inside each colored sheet.

4. Put the cardboard in bright sunlight. Record the temperature under each color at one-minute intervals. Which color seems to be the best heat absorber? The worst?

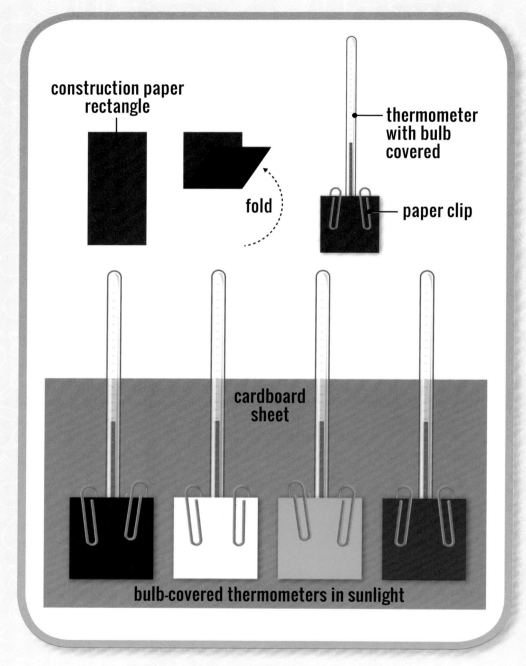

Figure 15. How does color affect solar heating?

FOR A SCIENCE IDEAS FAIR PROJECT

• Place equal weights of soils of different colors in bright sunlight. Which soil warms fastest?

• Place equal weights of clear water and water colored with black ink in identical containers. Place both in bright sunlight. Which is the better heat absorber?

• Carry out experiments to show how colored clothing can make you warmer or cooler.

4.9 **How the Wind Blows**

> ## THINGS YOU WILL NEED:
> - a balloon

Wind is the movement of air over Earth's surface. For anything to move, a force must act on it.

1. To discover what causes air to move, fill a balloon with air. Seal the neck of the balloon with your fingers. With your other hand, feel the balloon's surface. Do you feel an opposing force? Is the pressure greater inside or outside the balloon?

2. Put the balloon's mouth near your face. Slightly release your grip on the balloon's neck. You will feel a wind moving against your face. Why do you think air is flowing out of the balloon?

As you have just seen, air is pushed from high pressure to low pressure. But why are there differences in pressure? The reason is that the sun's heat is not spread evenly across Earth's surface. Tropical regions receive much more solar heat than polar regions. Consequently, tropical air is warmer than polar air.

As you know, warm air is less dense (lighter) and so it exerts less pressure. Higher pressure air then moves into the region of lower pressure.

If we lived on a frictionless planet that did not rotate, pressure differences alone could account for wind speed and direction. However, we live on a planet that turns and where friction is common. As a result, there is more to wind than just pressure differences.

4.10 Winds on Planet Earth

> ## THINGS YOU WILL NEED:
>
> - ball
> - shears
> - cardboard
> - turntable, piano stool that can spin, or lazy Susan
> - tape
> - felt-tip pen
> - a partner
> - ruler or yardstick

A rolling ball slows down and eventually stops because of friction. Friction is a force that opposes motion. Friction between the ball and the surface over which it rolls acts against the ball's motion. Air moving over the earth rubs against trees, grass, water, buildings, and so on. The air's velocity, like that of a rolling ball, is reduced by the friction.

In addition to pressure and friction, there is something else that affects winds. It is known as the Coriolis effect; it is caused by Earth's rotation. It was discovered by the French physicist Gaspard-Gustave de Coriolis (1792–1843) in 1835.

To understand this effect, think about the ground at the North Pole. It simply turns in place. It has no speed.

At the equator, the ground moves from west to east at a high speed. The equator is 24,900 mi (40,086 km) long, and Earth turns once every 24 hours. Therefore, anything on the equator moves eastward at 1,038 mi/hr (1,670 km/hr) because:

$$\frac{24{,}900 \text{ mi}}{24 \text{ hr}} = 1{,}038 \text{ mi/hr} \quad \text{or} \quad \frac{40{,}086 \text{ km}}{24 \text{ hr}} = 1{,}670 \text{ km/hr}$$

To see how the Coriolis effect affects winds, you can do an experiment.

1. Cut a piece of cardboard to match the circular top of a turntable, lazy Susan, or piano stool that can spin. Tape the cardboard to the surface on which you place it. The center of the cardboard represents Earth's North Pole. Its circumference represents Earth's equator.

2. Use a moving felt-tip pen to represent the path of wind moving from the North Pole toward the equator. Draw a straight line or radius from the center of the cardboard to its edge. That is the path winds might follow on a stationary Earth.

3. Have a partner slowly turn the cardboard counterclockwise (west to east) as seen from the North Pole. As the cardboard turns, slowly draw a straight line across its surface. Hold a ruler or yardstick just above the cardboard. The ruler will make sure you move the pen along a straight line. Keep the ruler fixed as you pull the pen along its side. How does this line compare with the previous one? Why is the line curved relative to the cardboard? Did it curve to the right or the left as it moved from pole to equator?

4. Repeat the experiment on a turning "Earth." This time draw a straight line from the edge (equator) of the circle to the center (North Pole). Again, you'll see that the line is curved and seems to bend. Did it bend toward the right or the left as it moved?

Why do the straight lines that you drew appear as curved lines on the rotating cardboard?

Winds moving across Earth's Northern Hemisphere appear to bend to the right just as the pen did when you pulled it in a straight line across the rotating disk. In the Southern Hemisphere, the winds bend to the left. Can you explain why?

Water currents in the ocean, such as the Gulf Stream, also bend due to Earth's rotation. Both winds and ocean currents bend to the right of their apparent path in the Northern Hemisphere (to the left in the Southern Hemisphere).

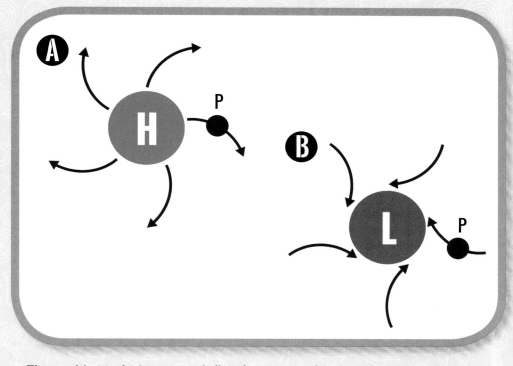

Figure 16. Winds (moving air) flow from areas of high pressure toward areas of low pressure. In the Northern Hemisphere, the Coriolis effect causes winds to curve to the right. The combination of these two factors causes air at points P to move clockwise around a high-pressure system (a) and counterclockwise around a low-pressure system (b).

Wind directions are affected by the Coriolis effect as well as air pressure differences. As a result, winds in the Northern Hemisphere move clockwise about a high pressure center. They move counter-clockwise about a low pressure center. See Figure 16.

To find the direction to a high or low pressure center, you can use Buys-Ballot's law. Stand with your back to the wind. Raise both arms so they are horizontal. Your right hand will point toward higher pressure. Your left hand will point toward lower pressure.

Chapter 5

Climate Change

It's a fact. The average temperature of planet Earth is rising. Slowly but surely, the globe is getting warmer than it has ever been. Today's global temperature is reported by how it compares to periods of time in the past. The annual temperature of the planet between 1951 and 1980 was about 14°C (57.2°F). In 2016, the hottest year in recorded history, the temperature was about 1°C (1.8°F) warmer than the period of 1951–1980. Today, global temperature change is accelerating.

Since 1997, the world has experienced the eighteen warmest years on record. Consider the Northern Hemisphere. Here the northernmost range of animal species is increasing by approximately 4 mi per decade. Springlike activities, such as the blossoming of plants and the arrival of migrating birds, are advancing by two to three days per decade. Frost depths are decreasing. Arctic winters are 2.2°C (4.0°F) warmer than they were fifty years ago. More than 1,200 cubic miles of glaciers have melted. During the last decade of the twentieth century, sea levels rose at an annual rate of 3 mm. For the previous 150 years, they had been rising at about 1 mm per year. The rise in sea level is the result of warmer seas and melting glaciers. From your knowledge of thermometers you know that liquids expand when warmed. Consequently, warmer oceans have grown deeper. Water from melting land glaciers flows into the oceans. This also causes them to expand. In the Arctic Ocean, 400,000 square miles of sea ice have disappeared since 1970. However, this loss of ice has not raised sea levels. To see why, try Experiment 5.1.

5.1 Glaciers and Sea Ice

> ## THINGS YOU WILL NEED:
> - 2 identical, clear, tall plastic cups or jars
> - water
> - ice cubes
> - marking pen
> - funnel

1. Find two identical, clear, tall plastic cups or jars. Add water to both until they are about half full.

2. Add two large ice cubes to one cup. These cubes represent sea ice, such as the ice floating on the Arctic or Southern Oceans. Use a marking pen to mark the water level in the cup.

3. Place a funnel in the second cup and mark the water level.

4. Add two large ice cubes to the funnel. This ice represents the ice in glaciers that rest on land. The funnel's spout represents rivers leading to the ocean.

5. When the ice has melted, look at the water levels in each cup. In which has the water level risen?

   Why won't melting sea ice raise the level of the oceans?

   If all the Arctic sea ice were to melt, it would have no effect on sea level. However, if the Greenland glaciers melted, sea level would rise an estimated 7 m (23 ft).

Global Warming

Earth's surface is warmed by the sun, the atmosphere, and slightly by Earth's own hot interior. It may surprise you to learn that the atmosphere helps to keep us warm. Most of the visible and ultra-violet light from the sun passes through our atmosphere and is absorbed by Earth's surface. These shorter wavelengths of light energy warm Earth. Some of that heat is radiated back into the atmosphere as longer wavelengths of infrared light.

The atmosphere contains greenhouse gases—carbon dioxide (CO_2), methane (CH_4), nitrous oxide (N_2O), sulfur hexafluoride (SF_6), chlorofluorocarbons, and water vapor (H_2O), which varies with humidity. These gases absorb infrared radiation and reradiate some of it back to Earth. In this way our atmosphere acts as a blanket, keeping Earth much warmer than it otherwise would be.

Since the Industrial Revolution, the amount of carbon dioxide in Earth's atmosphere has been increasing. For 10,000 years prior to that period, the concentration of greenhouse gases had been quite constant. (Ancient concentrations of atmospheric gases can be determined from air bubbles in ice cores drilled from glaciers.) Examine the graph in Figure 17a. It shows how atmospheric concentrations of carbon dioxide have been increasing. The graph, known as the Keeling curve, is named for Charles Keeling (1928–2005). He began measuring atmospheric carbon dioxide from the top of Mount Mauna Loa in Hawaii in 1958. His 1958 measurement was 316 ppm. (A concentration of 316 ppm means that every million molecules of gas in the atmosphere contains 316 molecules of carbon dioxide.) Today, that concentration is a little more than 400 ppm.

As you can see, the graph has a zigzag shape, which is a seasonal effect. During spring and summer in the Northern Hemisphere, atmospheric carbon dioxide decreases. Green plants are busily taking in carbon dioxide and water to make starch. The plants release oxygen as a by-product. This process, called photosynthesis, reduces the concentration of carbon dioxide in the atmosphere. During the winter, plants are less active. The carbon dioxide level rises again. But each winter it rises to a higher concentration than in the previous winter. This is made clearer by Figure 17b. It shows CO_2 concentrations for the period from January 1988 to January 1989. During that time, the CO_2 concentration increased from 350 to more than 352 ppm.

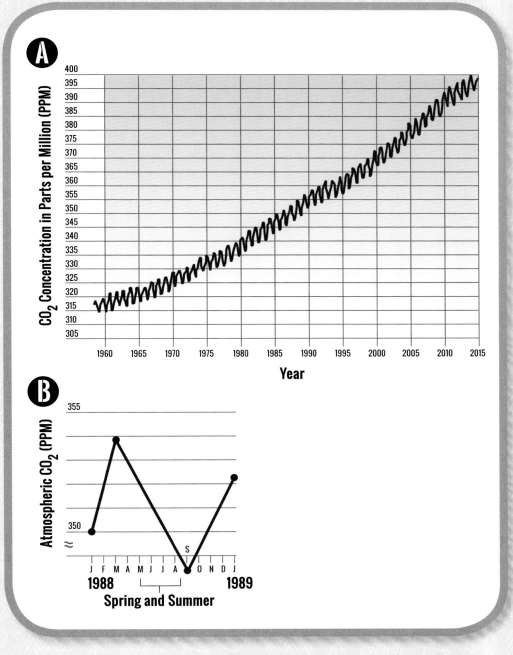

Figure 17. a) The Keeling curve. b) A detailed look at carbon dioxide concentrations during a one-year period.

Why doesn't the increased carbon dioxide produced during the Southern Hemisphere's summer balance out the Northern Hemisphere's winter? If you look at a globe, you will see that Earth's land, where plants grow, is predominantly north of the equator. As a result, summers south of the equator have a much smaller effect on atmospheric carbon dioxide.

Before the Industrial Revolution, the atmospheric concentration of carbon dioxide was 280 ppm. Today, that concentration is about 400 ppm. This means that 0.04 percent of atmospheric molecules are carbon dioxide. This is a very small quantity when compared with oxygen and nitrogen. Those gases make up 21 percent and 78 percent, respectively, of the atmosphere. However, as Figure 17a reveals, the concentration of atmospheric carbon dioxide has risen by approximately 23 percent since 1960. It has risen nearly 40 percent since the Industrial Revolution. The increase in atmospheric carbon dioxide is the primary cause of global warming. Its effect is compounded by the fact that it remains in the air for a long time. Furthermore, the atmospheric concentration of this gas grew more in the 1990s than in any decade since 1958. This coincides with the rapid industrialization of giant nations such as China and India. However, the United States emits more than one-fifth of the world's greenhouse gases into the atmosphere. Compare the fraction of the world's greenhouse gases produced by the United States with its fraction of the world's population (325 million to 7.4 billion).

Experiment 5.2 will show you how carbon dioxide affects an atmosphere.

5.2 A Greenhouse Gas

THINGS YOU WILL NEED:

- two 12-ounce cans of cola
- pitcher or measuring cup
- bright, warm, sunny day
- funnel
- 2 empty, clean, clear 2-liter plastic soda bottles
- identical thermometers
- modeling clay
- marking pen
- clock or watch
- notebook
- pen or pencil
- graph paper

In this experiment you will prepare two different atmospheres. One will contain a large amount of carbon dioxide. The other will contain much less carbon dioxide. You will then determine which atmosphere reaches a higher temperature when exposed to bright sunshine. The sun will heat the liquids in both bottles. The warm liquids will emit infrared radiation.

1. Obtain two 12-ounce cans of cola. Cola contains dissolved carbon dioxide. Pour the contents of one can into a pitcher or measuring cup. Leave this cola overnight. It will lose its carbonation (carbon dioxide) and become flat. Place the other sealed can of cola beside the opened cola so that both will be at about the same temperature.

2. On the next bright, warm, sunny day, open the other can of cola. Use a funnel to pour it into an empty, clean, clear 2-liter plastic soda bottle. Seal the bottle. Then shake the bottle vigorously to create a carbon dioxide atmosphere in the bottle.

3. Pour the pitcher or cup of flat cola into a second identical plastic bottle.

4. Place identical thermometers in the necks of both bottles. Use modeling clay to seal the mouths of the bottles and hold the thermometers firmly in place (see Figure 18a). You now have a rich carbon dioxide (CO_2) atmosphere in one bottle. Ordinary air with a little CO_2 will be in the other bottle. Use a marking pen to mark the bottle with the CO_2 atmosphere so you can identify it.

5. Place the bottles side by side in bright sunshine.

6. Record the temperature in each bottle at one-minute intervals until the temperatures stop rising.

7. Plot a graph of temperature versus time for each atmosphere. Both plots can be done on the same graph.

8. The graph in Figure 18b shows sample results for this experiment. How do those results compare with yours?

Carbon Dioxide Sources

Small amounts of carbon dioxide have been in Earth's atmosphere as long as life has existed on Earth—about 3 billion years. When living organisms respire, they take in oxygen and release carbon dioxide. Atmospheric oxygen used up through respiration is replenished by green plants during photosynthesis. In the natural world, the concentrations of carbon dioxide and oxygen are constant. The increased concentration of atmospheric carbon dioxide is the result of human activities. It is primarily the result of burning fossil fuels, such as coal, oil, and natural gas.

One gallon of gasoline (assume it is octane), burned to power a truck or car, produces 8.2 kilograms (18 pounds) of carbon dioxide. Automobiles and light trucks in the United States consume 150 billion gallons of gasoline each year. This results in the discharge of 1.2 trillion kilograms (2.7 trillion pounds) of carbon dioxide into the atmosphere. Each ton of coal burned in a power plant releases 3.67 tons of carbon dioxide into

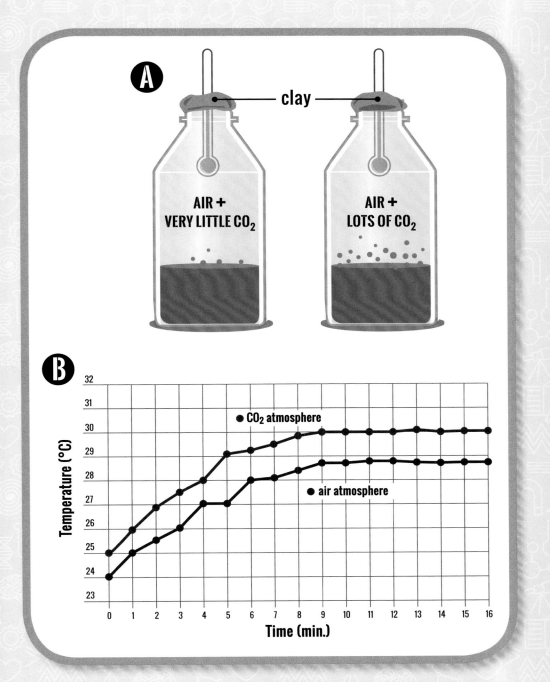

Figure 18. a) Two "atmospheres" in two bottles. b) Graph of temperature versus time for the two "atmospheres."

the air. Fossil fuel burning worldwide adds 27 trillion kilograms (59 trillion pounds) of carbon dioxide to the atmosphere each year.

Reducing Carbon Dioxide in the Atmosphere

Growing more trees could reduce atmospheric carbon dioxide levels by 10 to 15 percent. These plants would carry on photosynthesis and thus take in more CO_2 from the air. Unfortunately, the trend is in the other direction. Vast areas of the South American rain forest are being removed by logging, mining, and farming operations.

Another suggestion is to pump CO_2 into the ocean. But this would make the water more acidic. It would destroy coral reefs that nourish ocean life. It may be possible to bury carbon dioxide deep within Earth. However, the technology needed to do this is yet to be developed. Of course, the best solution is to develop alternative sources of energy. These include wind, solar, geothermal, tidal, wave, water, and nuclear energy (if a safe means of transporting and processing or storing nuclear waste can be developed).

The idea of pumping more CO_2 into the oceans is made difficult by the rise of water temperatures. Experiment 5.3 will help you to see why.

5.3 Carbon Dioxide and Seas

THINGS YOU WILL NEED:
- 2 cans of cola
- refrigerator

Carbon dioxide is soluble in water. More than 171 g of CO_2 will dissolve in 100 cm^3 of cold water. But ocean water is growing warmer as a result of global warming. What effect does this have on the solubility of carbon dioxide?

1. To find out, obtain two cans of a carbonated beverage, such as cola. Such beverages contain dissolved carbon dioxide.

2. Put one can in a refrigerator for several hours; leave the other can at room temperature.

3. Open the cold can. Then open the warm can. What happens?

   What do the results of this experiment tell you about temperature and the solubility of carbon dioxide? How will the solubility of carbon dioxide in ocean water be affected by global warming?

   The solubility of all gases, including oxygen, is affected in the same way by higher temperature. What effect may rising ocean temperatures have on fish, who take in oxygen from the water?

5.4 Evaporation and Global Warming

THINGS YOU WILL NEED:

- **an adult**
- 2 identical saucepans
- metric measuring cup
- cold water
- stove
- thermometer
- clock or watch

As you know, the water cycle involves the evaporation of water into the air. It condenses and falls back to Earth as rain. How will global warming affect evaporation?

1. To find out, obtain two identical saucepans. Using a measuring cup, add 200 mL of cold water to both pans.

2. Put one pan on a stove. **Ask an adult** to turn on a heating element under the pan. The water is to be kept warm, but not hot. Put a thermometer in the water. Try to keep the temperature at approximately 40 to 50°C (100 to 120°F).

3. Put the other pan on a kitchen counter away from the stove.

4. Examine the water in both pans every ten minutes. When approximately half the water in the pan on the stove has disappeared, turn off the stove.

5. Pour the water from the pan that was on the stove into a measuring cup. What volume of water remains? How much water evaporated?

6. Pour the water from the pan that was on the counter into a measuring cup. What volume of water remains? How much water evaporated?

What can you conclude about the effect of temperature on evaporation? How will global warming affect the amount of moisture in the atmosphere?

5.5 Polar Regions and Global Warming

THINGS YOU WILL NEED:

- scissors
- shiny aluminum foil
- ruler
- graduated cylinder or metric measuring cup
- cold water
- 2 foam coffee cups
- 2 thermometers (only 1 is essential)
- pliers
- cardboard
- heat lamp

Global warming is reducing the ice and snow that covers much of Earth's polar regions. The loss of this ice and snow compounds the problem of global warming. An experiment will show you why.

1. Use scissors to cut out two square pieces of shiny aluminum foil, each 8 cm (3 in) on a side.

2. Pour 100 mL of cold water into each of two foam coffee cups. Place a thermometer in each cup. Be sure that the water temperature is very nearly the same in both cups.

3. Fold one aluminum square into a small lump. Squeeze it with a pair of pliers. Drop it into one cup of water. It should sink.

4. Cover the other cup with the other aluminum square. The shiny aluminum represents the ice and snow that covers much of the polar seas.

5. Put the two cups side by side on a piece of cardboard. Place a heat lamp about 15 cm (6 in) above the cardboard. Center the lamp over a point midway between the two cups. See Figure 19.

6. Let the heat lamp shine on the two cups until the temperature in the uncovered cup reaches approximately 35°C (95°F).

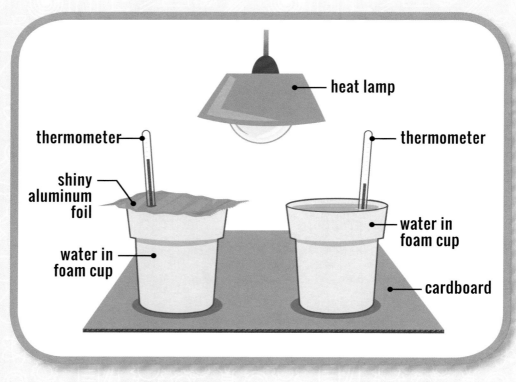

Figure 19. How does the loss of ice and snow affect global warming?

7. Turn off the lamp, remove the aluminum foil, and stir the water in both cups. Then read the two thermometers. What can you conclude? How does the loss of a reflecting surface of ice and snow compound global warming?

As you saw in this experiment, water reflects less light than aluminum foil. Remember that the foil was used to represent the snow and ice covering polar seas. Water reflects only 5 to 10 percent of the sunlight it receives. Ice and snow reflect 80 to 90 percent of sunlight. As Earth's snow and ice disappear, less solar energy is reflected back into space. Instead, Earth absorbs more sunlight and becomes even warmer. As melted glaciers flow to the ocean, sea levels will rise and add to coastal flooding.

Clouds, Aerosols, and Volcanoes

Factors that tend to reduce global warming are clouds, dust, and aerosols. Aerosols are particles in the air that come from forest fires, dust storms, volcanic eruptions, and the burning of fossil fuels. These particles reflect sunlight. This reduces the amount of solar energy that reaches Earth's surface. It counteracts global warming. Increased evaporation is expected to increase cloud cover and reduce solar heating. However, it will also increase the concentration of a potent greenhouse gas—water vapor. As a result, the effect of an increase in clouds is difficult to predict.

5.6 Clouds, Volcanoes, and Earth's Temperature

> ### THINGS YOU WILL NEED:
>
> - 2 clear plastic containers with clear, tight-fitting covers
> - 2 identical thermometers
> - clear tape
> - 2 strong rubber bands
> - wax paper
> - bright sunshine

In 1815, a volcano in Indonesia erupted, sending tons of volcanic ash, dust, and sulfur dioxide (SO_2) gas high into the atmosphere. The particles and gas spread around the globe, forming a thin cloud. The cloud reduced the amount of sunlight reaching Earth's surface. The following year became known in parts of the United States as the year without a summer.

The increase in volcanic dust and cloud cover was accompanied by an increase in aerosol droplets. These droplets contained sulfuric acid formed when the SO_2 combined with water vapor in the air. To see how the clouding affected global temperatures, you can do another experiment.

1. Find two clear plastic containers. Place identical thermometers in the containers as shown in Figure 20. Seal the containers with tight-fitting covers.

2. Cover one container with wax paper. The wax paper represents a thin cloud of volcanic ash and aerosols. Hold the wax paper in place with strong rubber bands. The other container represents a clear atmosphere.

3. Place both containers side by side in bright sunshine.

4. Wait until the temperature in the clear-covered container reaches 40°C (104°F) or stops rising. Then remove the wax paper cover. What was the temperature in the "dust-covered" atmosphere? What was the temperature in the clear atmosphere?

How would an atmosphere of volcanic ash, dust, and aerosols affect Earth's temperature?

Humans and Global Warming

How do we know human activity is causing global warming? Perhaps it is caused by an increase in the sun's energy output or by heat from Earth's core.

- First, the concentration of greenhouse gases is greatest over highly populated land in the Northern Hemisphere.
- Second, chemical analysis of isotopes in atmospheric carbon dioxide (CO_2) has been done. It shows that the CO_2 comes from burning fossil fuels. Methane and nitrous oxide come from agricultural waste as well as fossil fuels.
- Third, increases in global temperatures during the past decade agree with climate models developed by climatologists.
- Further, increases in atmospheric temperature are in the lower atmosphere (the troposphere). Upper atmosphere (stratosphere) temperatures are actually lower. Increased solar output would have the opposite effect.
- Ocean surface temperatures are increasing. Increased heat from Earth's core would raise temperatures deep within the oceans, not on the surface.

In 2014, the Intergovernmental Panel on Climate Change (IPCC) issued a report based on all the evidence. They concluded that the probability that global warming has been caused by human activity is greater than 90 percent.

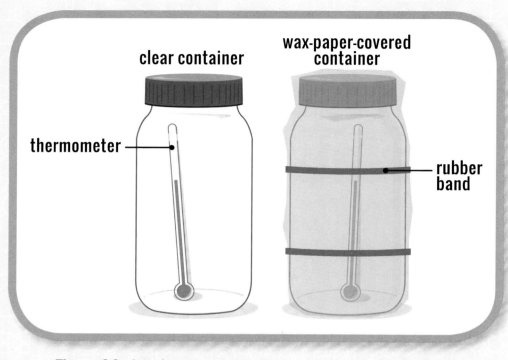

Figure 20 a) A clear "atmosphere." **b)** An "atmosphere" covered with "volcanic dust."

Scientists are using ever-improving models of climate. The models predict that global temperatures will increase by about 0.4°C (0.7°F) during the next two decades. Predictions for temperature increases during the twenty-first century range from 1.8 to 4.0°C (3.2 to 7.2°F). Temperature changes will depend on how much greenhouse gas emissions change. Again depending on emissions, oceans are expected to rise 30 to 40 cm (12 to 16 in). More than half the rise will be the result of thermal expansion. Melting glaciers in Greenland and Antarctica could add another 10 to 20 cm (4–8 in). We can also expect more precipitation, heat waves, and intense hurricanes. These climate changes will likely have further consequences. Tropical infectious diseases, such as malaria, will spread northward. Droughts and forest fires will increase. Rising sea levels will flood coastal-area homes and cities.

How Can Humans Combat Global Warming?

The best way to combat global warming is to reduce greenhouse gas emissions. This can only be done by reducing the burning of fossil fuels. There is evidence that this can be accomplished. Great Britain has proposed to reduce greenhouse gas emissions by 60 percent before 2050. Governments can require automobile makers to produce cars that go farther on a gallon of gasoline. Hybrid cars that get up to 60 miles per gallon are already on the roads.

Governments can support or engage in developing and expanding mass transportation—subways, buses, and trains. They can encourage people to walk or ride bikes. Tax incentives or penalties can hasten the development of renewable sources of energy.

Power plants need to move away from burning coal, oil, and natural gas to produce electrical energy. Alternative ways to generate electricity include using wind, solar, geothermal, tidal, wave, water, and nuclear energy sources.

There are also things that we as individuals can do to reduce global warming. We can buy smaller, more efficient cars. Walking or biking instead of driving will improve our health as well as reduce greenhouse gas emissions. We can use public transportation. We can conserve energy by using solar energy to heat water and buildings. Any new appliances (refrigerators, stoves, furnaces, and lightbulbs) should be energy efficient. Encourage towns and cities to use wind energy to power their facilities. Urge power companies to use green energy, such as wind and other renewable sources. If we all do our part, the effects of global warming can be lessened.

Science Supply Companies

Arbor Scientific
PO Box 2750
Ann Arbor, MI 48106-2750
(800) 367-6695
arborsci.com

Carolina Biological Supply Co.
PO Box 6010
Burlington, NC 27215-3398
(800) 334-5551
carolina.com

Connecticut Valley Biological
   Supply Co., Inc.
82 Valley Road
PO Box 326
Southampton, MA 01073
(800) 628-7748
ctvalleybio.com

Educational Innovations, Inc.
5 Francis J. Clarke Circle
Bethel, CT 06801
(203) 748-3224
teachersource.com

Fisher Science Education
300 Industry Drive
Pittsburgh, PA 15275
(800) 955-1177
fishersci.com

Frey Scientific
80 Northwest Boulevard
Nashua, NH 03061-3000
(800) 225-3739
freyscientific.com

Nasco
901 Janesville Avenue
Fort Atkinson, WI 53538
(800) 558-9595
enasco.com/science

Scientifics Direct
532 Main Street
Tonawanda, NY 14150
(800) 818-4955
scientificsonline.com

Ward's Science
5100 West Henrietta Road
PO Box 92912
Rochester, NY 14692-9012
(800) 962-2660
wardsci.com

Glossary

absolute humidity The mass of water vapor in a cubic meter of air.

air pressure The force per area exerted by air.

anemometer An instrument used to measure wind speed.

barometer An instrument used to measure air pressure.

Beaufort scale A way to estimate wind speeds by observing the effect of wind on objects, such as smoke, trees, leaves, and flags.

cloud A high concentration of small water droplets or ice crystals.

cohesion The attractive force between molecules, such as water molecules, that holds them together.

condensation The change of a gas into a liquid.

condensation nuclei Tiny particles on which water vapor can condense, forming water droplets.

Coriolis effect The effect of Earth's rotation on masses moving northward or southward over Earth's surface. The effect causes winds and ocean currents to bend to the right in the Northern Hemisphere and to the left in the Southern Hemisphere.

density The mass of a sample of matter divided by its volume.

dew point The temperature at which air becomes saturated with moisture and begins to condense.

evaporation The change of a liquid into a gas.

fog A cloud at ground level that forms when warm, humid air moves over a cold surface. The droplets are very small—2 to 50 microns (millionths of a meter).

global warming The slow increase in the temperature of Earth's air and water due to the increase of greenhouse gases in the atmosphere.

greenhouse gases Gases such as water vapor and carbon dioxide that reflect heat back to Earth's surface.

hygrometer An instrument used to measure relative humidity.

Keeling curve A graph showing the concentration of atmospheric carbon dioxide versus time from 1958 to the present.

meteorologist A scientist who studies weather.

precipitation Water deposited from the air as rain, hail, sleet, snow, dew, or frost.

pressure Force per area.

rainbow A spectrum of colors from violet to red that forms in the sky when sunlight is refracted and reflected by raindrops.

rain gauge An instrument used to measure rainfall in inches or centimeters.

relative humidity The mass of water vapor in a cubic meter of air compared with the amount it would hold if it were saturated with water vapor. It is usually expressed as a percent.

sling psychrometer An instrument used to measure relative humidity. It consists of two thermometers. One thermometer has a dry bulb; the bulb of the other thermometer is wet. The temperature difference between the two bulbs can be used to determine the relative humidity of the air.

temperature A measure of hotness or coldness.

temperature scales There are several temperature scales. The fixed points of the Celsius scale are the freezing temperature of water (0°C) and the boiling temperature of water (100°C), both at sea level pressure. The Fahrenheit scale uses the same fixed points but assigns them different values: 32°F for the freezing point and 212°F for the boiling point.

terminal velocity The steady velocity reached by a falling object. It occurs when air resistance equals the object's weight.

thermometer An instrument used to measure temperature. It is commonly used in weather stations to measure air temperatures.

vacuum An empty space where the pressure is zero.

vacuum pump A pump that can remove air from a container to create a vacuum.

water cycle The movement of water from Earth to air by evaporation and back to Earth as rain. The annual mass of water evaporated and the annual mass of rainfall are equal.

weather maps Maps that use symbols and lines to indicate temperatures, pressures, winds, precipitation, and weather fronts.

weather (wind) vane An instrument used to measure wind direction.

wind The movement of air over Earth's surface. Winds spread warm and cold air across the world.

wind direction The direction from which the wind is coming.

Further Reading

Books

Barrett, Raymond E. *The Annotated Build-It-Yourself Science Laboratory.* San Francisco, CA: Maker Media, 2015.

Buczynski, Sandy. *Designing a Winning Science Fair Project.* Ann Arbor, MI: Cherry Lake Publishing, 2014.

Garbe, Suzanne. *Living Earth: Exploring Life on Earth with Science Projects.* North Mankato, MN: Capstone Press, 2016.

Harris, Tim, ed. *Earth Science.* New York, NY: Cavendish Square, 2016.

Latta, Sara. *All About Earth: Exploring the Planet with Science Projects.* North Mankato, MN: Capstone Press, 2016.

Riechmann, Annie. *Whatever the Weather: Science Experiments and Art Activities That Explore the Wonders of Weather.* Boulder, CO: Roost Books, 2016.

Shea, Therese. *Freaky Weather Stories.* New York, NY: Gareth Stevens Publishing, 2016.

Sneideman, Joshua, and Erin Twamley. *Renewable Energy: Discover the Fuel of the Future with 20 Projects.* Whiter River Junction, VT: Nomad Press, 2016.

Sohn, Emily. *Experiments in Earth Science and Weather.* North Mankato, MN: Capstone Press, 2016.

Websites

Sci Jinks: Weather
scijinks.jpl.nasa.gov
Articles and news about weather, profiles of fun weather jobs, mobile games about satellites and technology, and exciting videos are available on this government website.

The Weather Channel
weather.com
Photos, weather maps, radar, and video give you the latest news about weather around the world.

Weather Wiz Kids
weatherwizkids.com
Learn more about the fascinating world of weather.

Index

A

absolute humidity, 54, 59–60
aerosols, 99, 100, 101
agricultural waste, 101
Agriculture, Department of, 75
air pressure, 9–24, 42, 45, 64, 75, 77, 85
alcohol, 7, 45, 67
alcohol thermometers, 7, 45
altocumulus clouds, 63
altostratus clouds, 63
anemometers, 52
aneroid barometers, 11, 20–24
Aristotle, 12
atmospheric carbon dioxide, 88, 90, 92, 94, 101

B

balloons, 75, 82
barometers, 9–11, 17–19, 20–24, 42, 62, 74
Beaufort scale, 52
Beaufort, Sir Francis, 52
boiling point, 45
British Navy, 52
Buys-Ballot's law, 85

C

carbonation, 91, 95
carbon dioxide, 16, 88, 90, 91, 92, 94, 95, 101
Celsius, Anders, 45
chlorofluorocarbons, 88
cirrocumulus clouds, 63
cirrostratus clouds, 63
cirrus clouds, 62, 63
climate change, 86–103
climatologists, 101

cloud cover, 62, 99, 100
clouds, 5, 20, 27, 48, 54, 62–65, 66, 74, 99, 100
cold fronts, 77, 78
Commerce, Department of, 75
compasses, 51
condensation, 5, 27, 30, 54, 59, 63, 65, 66, 96
condensation nuclei, 65, 66
controlled experiments, 8
Coriolis effect, 83, 85
Coriolis, Gaspard-Gustave de, 83
cumulonimbus clouds, 62, 63
cumulus clouds, 62

D

density, 16, 67, 68, 82
Department of Agriculture, 75
Department of Commerce, 75
dependent variables, 8
dew points, 42, 54, 59–61
digital thermometers, 45
diseases, 102
dot-dash system, 75
droughts, 102
dust storms, 99

E

eclipses, 62, 74
emissions, 102, 103
energy-efficient appliances, 103
evaporation, 25, 27, 28, 96, 99

F

Fahrenheit, Gabriel Daniel, 45
Ferdinand III, 12
fog, 63, 66, 72
forest fires, 99, 102
fossil fuels, 92, 94, 99, 101, 103

Franklin, Benjamin, 74
freezing point, 45
friction, 34, 82, 83
fronts, 77, 78
frost point, 60

G

geothermal energy, 94, 103
glaciers, 86, 87, 88, 98
global warming, 87–103
graphs, 47–48, 70, 88, 92
gravity, 27, 30, 34
green energy, 103
greenhouse gases, 88, 90, 91, 99,
    101, 102, 103
Gulf Stream, 74, 84

H

Halley, Edmond, 25
halos, 62
heat waves, 102
helium, 16, 75
helium balloons, 75
Henry, Joseph, 74–75
humidity, 30, 42, 52, 54, 55–60, 62,
    65, 66, 75, 88
hurricanes, 102
hybrid cars, 103
hydrogen balloons, 75
hydrographers, 52
hygrometers, 42
hypotheses, 7–8, 12

I

independent variables, 8
Industrial Revolution, 88, 90
infectious diseases, 102
infrared radiation, 88, 91
instruments, 42–61

Intergovernmental Panel on Climate
    Change (IPCC), 101
isobars, 77
isotherms, 77
isotopes, 101

K

Keeling, Charles, 88
Keeling curve, 88

L

lunar eclipses, 62, 74

M

Magdeburg hemispheres, 12
malaria, 102
mare's tails, 62
mercury, 7, 9, 11, 19, 45
meteorologists, 11, 38, 42, 52, 62
methane, 88, 101
Morse, Samuel F. B., 75

N

National Oceanic and Atmospheric
    Administration (NOAA), 75
National Weather Service, 75
nimbostratus clouds, 63
nitrogen, 16, 90
nitrous oxide, 88, 101
nor'easters, 74
Northern Lights, 62
nuclear energy, 94, 103

O

oxygen, 16, 88, 90, 92, 95

P

photosynthesis, 88, 92, 94
psychrometers, 42, 55, 59, 60

R

radiation, 88, 91
radio signals, 75
rain, 25–41, 42, 61, 62, 63, 64, 72, 96
rainbows, 62, 72–73
rain forests, 94
rain gauges, 38–40, 42, 62
relative humidity, 54, 55–58, 59, 60
relay, 74–75
renewable sources, 103
respiration, 92

S

safety rules, 6–7
satellites, 75
science fair projects, ideas for, 5–6, 16, 21, 24, 29, 31, 35, 37, 46, 48, 51, 60, 65, 71, 81
scientific method, 7–8
sea levels, 9, 11, 45, 86, 87, 98, 102
Signal Corps, 75
sling psychrometers, 42, 55, 59, 60
Smithsonian Institution, 75
snow, 36–37, 41, 62, 63, 71, 97, 98
snowflakes, preserving, 36–37
solar energy, 94, 98, 99, 103
stationary fronts, 77
stratocumulus clouds, 63
stratus clouds, 62, 63
sulfur dioxide, 100
sulfur hexafluoride, 88
sulfuric acid, 100

T

telegraph, 74–75
temperature scales, 45, 46
temperatures, graphing, 47–48
terminal velocity, 34, 35

thermometers, 7, 36, 42, 43–45, 46, 47, 55, 59, 60, 62, 70, 78, 86, 91, 92, 96, 97, 98, 100
thunderstorms, 54, 62, 74
tidal energy, 94, 103
Torricelli, Evangelista, 9, 12, 17

U

ultraviolet light, 87
updrafts, 54

V

vacuum, 9, 12, 14, 15, 16, 32, 33
vacuum pumps, 12, 14, 15, 16
vanes, 49–51, 74
variables, 8
velocity, 34, 35, 83
visible light, 87
volcanoes, 99, 100
von Guericke, Otto, 12, 14

W

warm fronts, 77
water cycle, 25–27, 96
water energy, 94, 103
wave energy, 94, 103
Weather Bureau, 75
weather fronts, 77, 78
weather instruments, 42–61
weather maps, 75–78
weather satellites, 75
weather stations, 38, 42, 74–75
weather (wind) vanes, 49–51, 74
wind energy, 94, 103
wind socks, 51